ECONOMIC BEHAVIOR
OF
ELECTRIC UTILITIES

PRENTICE-HALL SERIES IN ENERGY

W.J. Kennedy and W.C. Turner, *editors*

Gibson, *Energy Graphics*
Murphy and Soyster, *Economic Behavior of Electric Utilities*

ECONOMIC BEHAVIOR
OF
ELECTRIC UTILITIES

FREDERIC H. MURPHY
Temple University
Philadelphia, Pennsylvania

ALLEN L. SOYSTER
Pennsylvania State University
University Park, Pennsylvania

PRENTICE-HALL, INC., *Englewood Cliffs, New Jersey 07632*

Editorial/production supervision and
  interior design: Virginia R. Huebner
Cover design: Jeannette Jacobs
Manufacturing buyer: Anthony Caruso

Library of Congress Catalog Card Number   83-60613

Printed in the United States of America

10 9 8 7 6 5 4 3 2 1

ISBN   0-13-224089-0

Prentice-Hall International, Inc., *London*
Prentice-Hall of Australia Pty. Limited, *Sydney*
Editora Prentice-Hall do Brasil, Ltda., *Rio de Janeiro*
Prentice-Hall Canada Inc., *Toronto*
Prentice-Hall of India Private Limited, *New Delhi*
Prentice-Hall of Japan, Inc., *Tokyo*
Prentice-Hall of Southeast Asia Pte. Ltd., *Singapore*
Whitehall Books Limited, *Wellington, New Zealand*

This book is dedicated to
Ruth and Sharon

CONTENTS

PREFACE

The purpose of this book is to assess one aspect of the Midterm Energy Market Model (MEMM) electric utility submodel of the Department of Energy: the impact of incorporating the Averch-Johnson theory, a theory which was developed to analyze the behavior of a regulated monopoly subject to a rate-of-return constraint.

In Chapter 1 we shall examine the effect of two different theories on how electric utilites choose their equipment. These theories lead to different forecasts of electric utility fuel consumption, equipment selection, and prices. Chapter 2 contains explanations of what a public utility is and the economic rationale for regulation. There is also a summary of the legal history of regulation and the methods employed. Chapter 3 includes the model and a mathematical statement of the thesis developed by Averch and Johnson, and important subsequent analytical work is also described. The latter is linked to the problems of incorporating the Averch-Johnson hypothesis in a model of utility behavior in which the production function is not differentiable. Some empirical tests of Averch-Johnson are surveyed in Chapter 4. We find that the results of the empirical work are at best inconclusive and discuss comments by executives in regulated industries and alternative theories of regulation. The theoretical problems and practical consequences of extracting a submodel from a larger model are described in Chapter 5, along with how the Averch-Johnson thesis is implemented. Chapter 6 includes a detailed description of the results from the models. The initial results of this chapter show that the Averch-Johnson thesis with only rate-of-return control does not seem reasonable. Consequently, the Averch-Johnson theory is extended, assuming public utility commissions direct other decisions by utilities. Results of this extension of the Averch-Johnson model are then presented. Chapter 7 contains the overall conclusions of the study.

Special thanks are due Jalania Ellis for her tireless work in preparing the manuscript. Also, special acknowledgment goes to George Lady of Temple University and F. Thomas Sparrow of Purdue University who contributed thorough, careful, and thoughtful reviews. The responsibility for any remaining errors or omissions rests entirely with the authors.

FREDERIC H. MURPHY

ALLEN L. SOYSTER

ECONOMIC BEHAVIOR
OF
ELECTRIC UTILITIES

1

MODELING RESOURCE ALLOCATION DECISIONS BY ELECTRIC UTILITIES

Two economic theories are used to describe electric utility equipment selection decisions. The first theory is that electric utilities minimize the costs of meeting demand. The second theory is that electric utilities maximize profits subject to a rate-of-return constraint. The two theories lead to different consequences because costs are not minimized when there is a rate-of-return constraint.

The first theory, cost minimization, is sometimes perceived as a totally invalid theory of electric utility behavior, because there are seemingly no incentive structures that would lead a regulated monopoly to necessarily minimize costs. It is, however, the most common method for modeling utility behavior in policy models. The main reason for using this criterion is that in their models for planning individual utilities use this criterion for decision making; see, for example, Massé and Gibrat [34]. The second theory, known as the Averch-Johnson (A-J) theory [2], simply stated, concludes that for a given quantity of electricity produced the mix of equipment used would be more capital intensive than under cost minimization. Consequently, in forecasting utility behavior one would presume that more coal or nuclear facilities, as opposed to oil or gas, would be built under the A-J hypothesis.

The concern of Averch and Johnson, and the basic concern of most economists, is in searching for distortions in the economy that are counter to economic efficiency. Economic efficiency in production is achieved when the marginal cost of an input is equal to the value of its marginal product. An important attribute of cost minimization is that it leads to efficient solutions. In perfectly competitive markets, cost minimization coincides with profit maximization. The conclusions about a capital bias from the A-J hypothesis imply an economic inefficiency leading to higher costs of electricity. The original interest in the theory was to determine the extent to which prices are increased and to explore alternative regulatory procedures to reduce distortion. Since the 1973-1974 oil embargo, the theory has become important for its implications on fuel use patterns.

There is an extensive theoretical literature on the subject, and there is a growing empirical literature testing the validity of the A-J hypothesis. This literature is described in Chapter 3. Rather than try to expand the empirical tests using econometric techniques, the goal of this research is to examine the effects on fuel choices and energy consumption as influenced by alternative choices of the incentives faced by electric utilities.

AN APPROACH TO ESTIMATING THE IMPACT OF THE A-J INCENTIVE STRUCTURE

To see how different energy forecasts would compare under the two theories, the electric utilities submodel was extracted from the Midterm Energy Market Model (MEMM). This model has been used by the Energy Information Administration of the Department of Energy for constructing forecasts of supplies, demands, and prices of energy commodities. The submodel, as well as the entire MEMM model, is described in detail in Chapter 5. The electric utilities submodel presumes that utilities are cost minimizers. Forecasts using this model have been subject to criticism because of this assumption. Rather than testing for the presence of A-J behavior, this study is designed to examine the consequences of the two theories on electric utility behavior within the context of a single model. By studying how the model behaves, insight can be gained into how the A-J theory would appear in an operational setting.

Quantitative as well as qualitative results are produced. The qualitative results describe how the fuel consumption patterns will be different with the two theories. The quantitative results allow the determination of the importance of forecast differences. The question treated here is different from a comparative statics analysis in that existing capacity and lead times influence the results. The presence of an initial capital stock can lead to conclusions that are different from what the static theory predicts.

Even ignoring real-world uncertainties, the quantitative estimates presented here are one set of results in a wide range of possibilities. To a greater degree than with qualitative analysis, all quantitative results comparing the theories are contingent on the model structure. Another factor influencing the levels of the differences is the legislative environment under which utilities are presumed to operate. For example, when the best-available-control-technology (BACT) environmental regulations are combined with the Powerplant and Industrial Fuel Use Act (PIFUA), available options for new equipment are heavily circumscribed. The alternative forecasts become similar because the model is more an accounting of the regulations than a characterization of behavior. For this analysis, the environmental assumptions, in contrast to BACT, are that only high-sulfur coal requires scrubbing, gas use is restricted because of prohibitions during the 1970s, and the PIFUA is not restricting the choice of equipment. These policy assumptions were chosen to allow for the maximum possible difference between the A-J theory and cost minimization.

THE NATURE OF ELECTRIC UTILITIES

Electric utilities represent one of the major components of the energy sector. Forecasting their fuel choices is an important part of the total supply-demand picture. To give an idea of their role, in 1979 they consumed 11.3 quads of coal, 3.4 quads of oil, and 3.6 quads of natural gas, where a quad is a quadrillion British thermal unit. That is, in 1977 utilities consumed a total of 18.2 quads out of the 73.0 quads of fossil fuel consumed in the United States. Table 1 shows the importance of electrical generation to the energy sector of the economy and, therefore, to answering questions about the future of energy use in the United States.

Almost half of the overall cost of producing electricity is fuel cost. The other half is capital costs for new generating equipment, operating and maintenance costs for this equipment, and the costs of transmission and distribution. Although a major portion of utility costs are associated with transmission and distribution, this discussion emphasizes electricity generation because this is where the fuel choices are made.

Compared to manufacturing industries, utilities have a limited set of production technologies and a small product line. Currently, the generally available plants are light water nuclear reactors; coal, oil, or gas steam; gas or distillate turbines; gas or distillate combined cycle plants; and hydropower. A simple view of combined cycle plants is that they are combined turbine and steam plants where the waste heat from the turbines is used to generate steam.

TABLE 1   1979 U.S. Sectorial Fuel Consumption (Trillion Btu's)

Sector	Coal	Oil	Gas	Nuclear	Hydro, etc.[a]	Total
Residential	82	2,297	5,055	—	—	7,434
Commercial	129	2,307	2,836	—	—	5,272
Industrial	3,702	9,117	8,562	—	—	21,381
Transportation		19,851	612	—	34	20,463
Electric generation	11,263	3,357	3,609	2,748	3,221	18,229
Total	15,176	36,929	20,861	2,748	3,255	78,969

[a]Nuclear and hydro entries estimate the Btu consumption for an equivalent fossil fuel plant at 10,000 Btu/kWh.

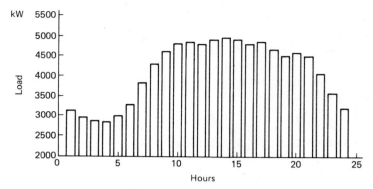

Figure 1   Daily load curve.

The dominant characteristic of electric utilities is that they cannot easily inventory their product to meet fluctuations in demand. Currently, the only economic way electricity can be produced to inventory is through pumped storage hydroelectric facilities. Here, when electricity demand is low, electric pumps are used to raise water behind a dam. The water is stored to meet peak electricity demands as potential energy and is reconverted to electricity as hydropower.

Even with pumped storage, electricity must be generated as needed. This means an important characteristic to be captured in modeling the behavior of electric utilities is demand fluctuations and how the demand fluctuations influence capacity selection. How demand varies over time can be represented by a load curve, as shown in Figure 1. Since the load is dependent on electricity-consuming equipment that performs specific functions, the demand at any moment is determined by the functions required. Air conditioning exaggerates the afternoon peak in summers, and home heating raises the evening-night

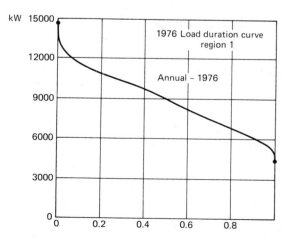

Figure 2   Annual load duration curve.

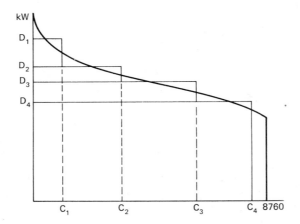

Figure 3　An approximation to the load curve.

consumption in winter. Because different functions are required at different times of the year, there are seasonal as well as daily peaks. Air conditioning leads to an overall summer peak for most utilities. However, recent penetration by electricity into home heating markets in certain regions has led to winter peaks as well as summer peaks in demand.

A useful aggregation of all the daily load curves occurring in a given year is termed the annual load duration curve and is illustrated in Figure 2. The annual load duration curve is a reordering of all the load curves by hourly demand. (There are 8760 hr/year.) The annual load curve is sorted in order of decreasing power demanded. Using this aggregation of demand fluctuations allows the discretization of demand into segments where capacity operates at different rates (see Figure 3). Here $C_1/8760$ is the fraction of time a demand level of D_1 must be met. The equipment designated to meet the increment of demand between D_1 and D_2 operates at a lower rate than the equipment assigned to meet the demand between D_2 and D_3.

Consequently, some of the equipment is operated to its limit, that is, with a high capacity factor. Other equipment is used a very small percentage of the time, perhaps only 10% of the time. For equipment operated at a high capacity factor, it is desirable to have a low fuel cost; for equipment rarely operated, it is important to have low capital costs. Therefore, utilities have a mix of equipment, with different plants used to meet different portions of the load. Figure 4 illustrates how different kinds of equipment are more economic at different operating rates, where the total cost consists of a fixed capital cost plus a variable operating cost. A plant with a low capital cost like A is more economic at a low capacity factor than a plant like C with a high capital cost but a low operating cost.

The major decisions associated with the generation facilities of electric utilities revolve around

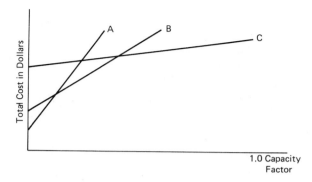

Figure 4 A breakeven chart showing which plant has the lowest capital plus operating cost for each capacity factor.

- Capital acquisition
- Equipment utilization (dispatching)
- Equipment availability (maintenance scheduling)

This simplified discussion ignores other concerns of utilities such as financing, contract structures for fuel acquisition, dealing with the regulatory processes, and all the aspects of transmission such as power wheeling and interties.

UTILITY DECISIONS WHERE THE AVERCH—JOHNSON EFFECT MAY OCCUR

There is a whole range of decisions where the A-J hypothesis may be realized. The most obvious area is within the design of a given plant. There may be excessive efficiency built into the design. The theoretical efficiency is between .5 and .6. That is, 1 Btu of fuel can be converted into .5 Btu of electricity. The actual efficiencies range from .3 to about .4. Incremental improvements in efficiencies involve substantially increasing capital investments. Under the A-J hypothesis a utility would build a plant with a higher thermal efficiency than a plant designed to minimize costs. Several of the studies described in Chapter 4 treat this aspect of utility decision making. However, these studies are necessarily incomplete as the optimal efficiency depends on the capacity factor, which varies over the life of the plant.

The most important decisions in determining energy forecasts that may be affected by the A-J hypothesis relate to fuel choices. Plant costs vary substantially with the fuel chosen because of the different physical properties of the fuels. In the extreme, a utility could choose the fuel that requires the largest capital expenditure. For example, comparing the relative costs of an oil versus coal plant as a function of capacity factor results in Figure 5. Because coal and oil plants have different capital and fuel cost ratios, with coal more capital intensive,

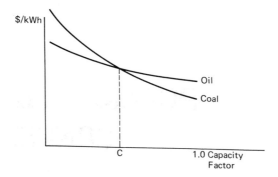

Figure 5 Comparison of costs as a function of capacity factor.

electricity from coal plants is cheaper than electricity from oil plants when the coal plant is operated with a high capacity factor. Concomitantly, with a low capacity factor the oil plant is cheaper to build and operate. At capacity factor c, both plants cost the same. The A-J effect could appear through having an inappropriate mix of equipment. That is, a utility could have so much coal capacity that some plants are operated with a capacity factor less than c. The larger capital investment in a coal plant leads to a greater capital investment than is consistent with cost minimization c. In this case, capital is substituted for fuel.

Having too much capacity is not necessarily evidence of the A-J effect. First, when planning for future capacity additions, the decisions are made without perfect foresight about demand. The costs of undercapacity to a utility tend to be greater than the costs of overcapacity, leading to overbuilding. Also, it is common to understate the rated design capacity due to penalties for not meeting a given contracted performance standard. This means that when a utility purchases a plant, it gains a specified minimum addition to capacity plus some uncertain quantity beyond the minimum.

There are other decisions that may be influenced by the A-J hypothesis. Examples are plant location and investment in transmission and distribution capacity. Mine-mouth generation reduces fuel costs while increasing transmission costs and the rate base. The layout of a plant and its planned reliability may save on labor, as opposed to fuel, leading to an expanded rate base. The A-J effect can appear in any decision involving a capital expenditure that reduces either fuel or labor costs.

In this book the emphasis is on the fuel choice decision. The fuel mix is important for energy policy analysis because electric utility demand for oil affects oil imports, and the demand for natural gas is a major determinant of natural gas prices throughout the country.

2

PUBLIC UTILITY
CONCEPTS

INTRODUCTION

The purpose of this chapter is to provide some background for studying the Averch-Johnson theory. A public utility is defined, and the history of regulation in the United States is discussed. Since the A-J model posits only one theory of utility behavior, some of the alternatives are presented.

Currently, it is not clear how the regulatory commissions behave, and it is not clear how effective they are. The A-J theory is the first truly analytical statement of the behavior of a firm under regulation. The conclusions from the theory form the basis of popular assumptions about utility actions. The intention here is to put the theory in perspective from the viewpoint of economic theory and regulatory practice.

DEFINITION OF A PUBLIC UTILITY

One can easily list several public utilities. Examples are the suppliers of some commodities that are considered necessities such as transportation, electricity, gas, and water. Furthermore, utilities are firms whose prices are closely watched and regulated by the government. Strangely, though, the precise definition of what constitutes a public utility, and what does not, is hard to comprehend. It is circular to define a public utility as a firm whose prices and output are subject to governmental regulation, because what is important in defining a public utility is that which makes regulation necessary: excessive market power.

One characteristic of public utilities, as seen by layman and economist alike, is that the utility supplies a service or good that is an absolute necessity of an industrialized society. Without electricity or water, any economic system, whether capitalistic or socialistic, could not possibly function. Nevertheless, there are other industries that provide necessary goods and services and do not have their profits regulated. No one would argue that food or even automobiles are not also necessary commodities in this or any other industrialized society. If public utility status were conferred upon every industry whose output is associated with some degree of necessity, then, apparently, only those firms that produce so-called *luxury* goods would escape the status as a public utility. In short, necessity of the service or good is a necessary but not sufficient condition for public utility status.

Another characteristic of public utilities is that huge amounts of capital are required to provide the service. Furthermore, the classical assumption is that utilities have decreasing, long-run average cost curves; that is, the nature of the technology leads to a situation in which the least cost configuration for providing the service is a monopoly. A situation in which three or four electric utilities serve the same city requires replication of generation, transmission, and distribution facilities. Imagine the difficulty and complexity of four different water companies laying in systems to serve subsets of customers on the same street. Hence, another characteristic of public utilities is that the inherent technology is one in which there are significant returns to scale. But this characteristic is not unique to gas, water, and electric companies. Steel, aluminum, and automobile industries possess similar properties. In the United States three aluminum companies (Alcoa, Reynolds, and Kaiser) dominate the industry, and the technology is highly capital intensive with tremendous returns to scale.

Bonbright [10] emphasizes a third characteristic of public utilities that differentiates them from other firms satisfying the first and second conditions. Public utilities serve restricted markets, because of the necessarily direct connection between the utility and the customer. The water line, the gas line, and the electric line physically link the supplier and consumer, a link that represents a significant investment. This delivery system, almost a universal characteristic of utilities, is what clearly differentiates the utility from an aluminum company. When Alcoa wants to penetrate the Los Angeles market area, there is no particular technological barrier. But this is not the case with Potomac Electric Power Company (PEPCO). PEPCO is destined to serve a local market in the Potomac River area.

As pointed out by Bonbright [10], public utilities are basically in the transmission and distribution business. To be sure, electric utilities also possess generating stations, but the transmission and distribution facilities are a vital part of the overall system. Moreover, many electric utilities deal only in the transmission and distribution end of the business.

In summary, the gas, water, and electric utilities possess all the following three characteristics: providing a necessity, operating with a high return to scale technology, and requiring a direct link between the supplier and customer. (Note also that the service provided cannot, in any significant quantity, be stored or deferred.) These characteristics clearly identify a framework in which allowing unregulated competition represents a potentially disastrous state of affairs with an unregulated monopoly in a position to extract exorbitant profits. What we see today is a substitute for competition. One firm is given an exclusive franchise to serve a particular region, but this firm has its profits regulated by the government. The *fair rate of return* determined by a governmental regulatory body is supposed to represent "a substitute for the beneficial aspects of competition."

LEGAL HISTORY

The legal basis for regulation rests ultimately in the U.S. Constitution and subsequent amendments. The so-called *commerce clause* states

> [Congress has the power] To regulate Commerce with Foreign nations, and among the several States, and with the Indian Tribes.

In addition, the *welfare clause* states

> The Congress shall have the power to lay and collect Taxes, Duties, Imposts and Excises, to pay Debts and provide for the common Defense and general welfare of the United States.

In terms of regulatory matters, another clause, the *elastic clause*, has also been important:

> To make all Laws which shall be necessary and proper for carrying into Execution the foregoing Powers, and all other Powers vested by this Constitution in the Government of the United States, or in any Department or Office thereof.

These three clauses have guided the Supreme Court opinions on economic regulation over the past 200 years.

One of the most important decisions of the Supreme Court concerning regulation is an 1877 case which involved a farmer's organization (Grange) and Munn and Scott, owners of grain elevators in Illinois. In 1871, the Illinois legislature passed a law which made all grain elevators public utilities and hence subject to governmental regulation. Munn and Scott did not follow the regulations and eventually appealed their subsequent arrest to the U.S. Supreme Court, based on the plea that they were involved simply in a private business.

What the Munn vs. Illinois case amounted to was a test of whether the government could regulate any business that "affected the public welfare." Since the U.S. Supreme Court upheld the Illinois legislature, it then became clear that any business which affects the public well-being is potentially subject to governmental regulation. In a dissenting opinion in Munn vs. Illinois, Justice Field said

> If this be a sound law . . . all property and all business in the State are held at the mercy of legislature. . . . The public is interested in cotton, woolen and silk fabrics, in the construction of machinery. . . .

Another notable decision of the U.S. Supreme Court involved Nebbia vs. New York in1933. This case involved a merchant who sold milk in his grocery store at a price below the minimum as set by the State of New York. This case, in which the New York law was upheld, is important from two points of view. First, the nature of the New York milk price controls was to protect producers, not consumers. Second, it affirmed the right of a state to regulate any business affecting the public interest.

Just as the economic definition of a public utility is not altogether clear, the same must be said of the legal definition. This is summarized by Farris and Sampson [21]:

> The courts have been somewhat erratic and inconsistent in applying the concept of "businesses affected with a public interest," and they now seem to have abandoned this function to legislative bodies. For practical purposes, then, it would not be far wrong to assume that a public utility is any business which an appropriate legislative body declares to be a public utility!

DIFFERING REGULATORY SCHEMES

Until the nineteenth century, the only recourse in a public utility matter for an individual, with a complaint about prices or service, was to proceed directly with the courts. This method was slow and ineffective. Furthermore, it was by definition an after-the-fact type of regulation. In the nineteenth century, regulation became part of the legislative process, both federal and state. A particular state would grant certain franchises to private business and in doing so stipulate certain operating conditions.

Regulation by legislation has many disadvantages. A principal disadvantage is the inherent loss of flexibility and ability to deal with changing business conditions. Furthermore, important details and contingencies in the franchise are often difficult and too technical for many legislators who are not intimately familiar with the business.

During the latter part of the 1800s, another approach to regulation evolved, the independent regulatory commission. The commission would be a group of individuals, appointed or directly elected, that would devote full time to managing the details of regulation, a surrogate for the legislatures themselves. At the federal level we have, for example, the Interstate Commerce Commission,

Civil Aeronautics Board, Federal Power Commission, and Federal Communications Commission. Counterparts to many of these federal commissions exist at the state level.

The commission type of regulation is the dominant form today. The alternative has many advantages. The independent commission provides continuous surveillance by full-time, professional regulators, supported by a staff of economists, lawyers, and accountants. The principal advantage of the commission is probably its flexibility to deal with a changing business climate and the concomitant problems of costs and prices. The flexibility is also, according to some, one of its weaknesses in that sometimes very broad powers are in the hands of very few.

CONTEMPORARY LEGAL STRUCTURES OF REGULATION

Electric utilities have their prices set by public utility commissions. These prices provide for a return on investment by the utilities. The problem addressed in this section is how the fair rate of return should be established for a private firm whose prices are being regulated by the government. In addition to setting an allowed rate of return, the value of the firm's assets must be established. The main emphasis is upon how, in past cases, the U.S. Supreme Court has interpreted the U.S. Constitution and the subsequent effect upon the workings of the various regulatory commissions.

Valuation of Assets

The necessary background required to understand the problems faced by the courts and various commissions is conceptually quite simple. Consider a hypothetical utility which, say, in 1950 raised $1000 and began supplying a certain service. By, say, 1960, the stock of the utility has a net value of $3000, although no new capital has been invested. This increase in value is attributed to at least two factors: The replacement cost of the equipment has increased, and the "going value" of the firm is formally acknowledged by investors. This value as a going concern arises because successful venture requires the coherent management of various components on enterprise such as capital, labor, and technology. How should the net worth of the firm be evaluated? At $1000 or $3000? Such a decision has important consequences for both the owners and the consumers of the service.

Although important court opinions relating to regulatory processes occurred during the early and mid-1800s, it is not unreasonable to begin with the celebrated Smyth vs. Ames case of 1898. The court ruling in this case was a dominant factor in regulatory decision making for the next 50 years. The opinion expressed in this case was that rate makers base their decisions on a percentage of the "fair value of property being used by it for the convenience of the public" [48]. The factors to be used in this determination were referenced as follows:

> . . . the original cost of construction, the amount expended in permanent improvements, the amount and market value of bonds and stocks, the present as compared with the original cost of construction, the probable earning capacity of the property under particular rates prescribed by the statute, and the sum required to meet operating expenses. . . .

The working interpretation of this Supreme Court ruling was that a mixture of both valuation methods, original and replacement, was appropriate and that the relative degree was discretionary.

A substantial portion of this opinion came under severe criticism in subsequent years. The circular reasoning was criticized. In particular, how can *probable earning capacity* be used to determine rates when allowed rates specify earning capacity? Nonetheless, this decision was a dominant force in rate-making proceedings, which became dominated with lengthy testimony be engineers in an effort to determine the *fair value of property*.

Various commissions and lower courts tended to favor the *reproduction cost* methods. The McCardle case, 1927 [36], is seen by some as the high point of this method. The Supreme Court said

> . . . Consideration must be given to prices and wages prevailing at the time . . . it must be determined whether the rates . . . are yielding and will yield . . . a reasonable rate of return on the value of the property at the time of the investigation and for a reasonable time in the future.

By 1942, the U.S. Supreme Court had come full circle and essentially freed the commissions of the court-imposed valuation methods. In reference to the 1942 Natural Gas Pipeline decision [23],

> The Constitution does not bind ratemaking bodies to the service of any single formula or combination of formulas. Agencies to whom this legislative power has been delegated are free, within the ambit of their statutory authority, to make the pragmatic adjustments which may be called for by particular circumstances. Once a fair hearing has been given, proper findings made, and other statutory requirements satisfied, the courts cannot intervene in the absence of a clear showing that the limits of due process have been overstepped. If the commission's order, as applied to the facts before it and viewed in its entirety, produces no arbitrary result, our inquiry is at an end.

One result of this expression was a clear lack of any useful guidelines for working commissions. Two years later, in the celebrated Hope decision [22], a new point of view was established by the U.S. Supreme Court, the so-called *end result* doctrine, which, to date, is the ruling expression of the U.S. Supreme Court:

> . . . It is the result reached, not the method employed, which is controlling. . . . It is not the theory but the impact of the rate order which counts. . . . Rates which enable the company to operate successfully, to maintain its financial integrity, to attract capital, and to compensate its investors for risks assumed certainly cannot be condemned as invalid, even though they might produce only a meager return on the so-called "fair value" rate base.

This ruling obviously interchanged the importance of rate base and rate of return. Leventhal [33] very elegantly summarized the impact of the Hope case as follows: "the role of 'rate of return' was elevated from that of a featured player to that of a star." Another excerpt from the majority Hope opinion is as follows:

> The investor has a legitimate concern with the financial integrity of the company whose rates are being regulated. From the investor or company point of view it is important that there be enough revenue not only for operating expenses, but also for the capital costs of the business. These include service on the debt and dividends of the stock. *By that standard, the return to the equity owner should be commensurate with returns on investments in other enterprises having corresponding risks. That return, moreover, should be sufficient to assure confidence in the financial integrity of the enterprise, so as to maintain its credit and attract capital.*

The italicized portion (italics are not included in the original passage) suggests two alternative, but not independent, methods for determining a fair rate of return:

- Comparable earnings
- Cost of capital

Determining a "Fair" Rate of Return

The *comparable-earnings* standard refers to setting a rate that results in earnings similar to that of other firms in the same risk class, while *attraction of capital* refers to that rate which ensures the longevity of the firm when viewed in the competitive capital markets. Both, of course, are a recognition that the firm must provide a return that is acceptable to investors who, otherwise, can take their capital elsewhere.

The role of these two criteria is illustrated in the case of the State Corporation Commission vs. the Federal Power Commission (involving Northern Natural Gas Company) in 1953. In this case, the Federal Power Commission (FPC) computed the *cost of capital* for Northern as follows:

$$56\% \text{ debt @ } 2.55\% = 1.43\%$$
$$44\% \text{ equity @ } 9.25\% = \underline{4.07\%}$$
$$5.50\%$$

where the 9.25% cost of equity was calculated as 8.75% plus .5% for flotation costs. The 8.75% was an estimate of the average earnings to price ratio for common stock shares of seven *other* gas companies with stock traded on a recognized exchange.

The Supreme Court overturned the FPC-determined 5.5% rate of return. The opinion was based on the fact that FPC witnesses in no way demonstrated that the risk category of Northern was similar to the other gas companies. Furthermore, the court pointed out that FPC witnesses testified that 5.75–6% rates were currently in effect with other gas companies. The court fixed the rate at 6%.

The approach most often used in determining the cost of equity capital (like the preceding example) is based on the capitalized future earnings of the regulated firm. Suppose that a firm can be expected to earn an amount X each year to perpetuity. At a discount rate d, the present value of this infinite stream is

$$V = \sum_{t=1}^{\infty} \frac{X}{(1+d)^t} = \frac{X}{d}$$

This basic formula leads to the valuation of d as

$$d = \frac{X}{V}$$

or

$$d = \frac{X}{np}$$

where n is the number of shares, p the current price, and $V = np$. This formula includes the tacit assumption that the stock price ultimately reflects the value of the firm. In the preceding case, the value of d was estimated via the (per share) ratio of earnings to price.

The criticism of the comparable-risk method of valuation is that investors buy prospective, not current, earnings and that this method neglects the principal component of market value, future earnings. Furthermore, transient effects and vagaries of the market make the application of this method less than straight-forward. Yet Leventhal [33] says

> . . . the technique of these ratios has continued to be the dominant, if not the sole, tool of analysis in a large number of cases. The technique required some judgment in application, but it has the line of apparent certitude and simplicity of calculation.

On the other hand, Leventhal argues that, contrary to opinions of some economists in the public utility field, in the leading cases involving regulation the primary *legal* standard is the comparable-earnings criterion. Leventhal cites a sequence of cases including Wilcox vs. Consolidated Gas [61], Bluefield Water Works vs. Public Service Commission [9], and Southwestern Bell vs. Public

Service Commission [49] in which the reference to comparable earnings was the chief legal argument.

In summary, we quote from Leventhal [33]:

> Regulatory commissions have, in fact, at least in the past decade, been applying substantial increases above the returns indicated by the capital-attracting testimony based on concurrent earning-price ratios that came into prominent use after Hope. Sometimes particular factors have been seized upon as justifying the increment. More often the commission has merely recognized the necessity of the application of generous judgment to the raw earnings-price data. I offer the hypothesis that what has transpired is that commissions, without expressly or even consciously invoking a comparable-earnings standard, have in fact used their own rough and ready awareness of comparable earnings available elsewhere as the principal component of judgment that enhances return to equity substantially above the capitalization rates derived from concurrent earnings-price ratios.

And so now public utility commissions (PUCs) combine asset valuation with a comparable-earnings estimate for a return on equity. According to the National Association of Regulatory Utility Commissions [39], the individual state public utility commissions currently value property as in Table 2 and include the items mentioned in Table 3. The allowed rates of return change regularly because of inflation and widely fluctuating interest rates.

REGULATORY THEORIES AND STRUCTURES

The most commonly held theory concerning the pattern of governmental regulation of private enterprise is the *public interest* concept. According to Posner [44], "This theory holds that regulation is supplied in response to the demand of the public for correction of inefficient or inequitable market practices." Posner suggests that this theory is "more assumed than articulated" and further characterizes the present state of affairs by adding that it is "a theory bequeathed by a previous generation of economists to a present generation of lawyers."

Posner further explains that one of the main underlying assumptions characterizing earlier viewpoints on government regulation is that some market imperfection was inherently present. In reference to electric utilities, this imperfection would be the near total lack of competition, that is, the existence of a monopolistic supplier. In this case, the public interest theory of regulation may seem justified, although Posner questions whether the evolution of regulation in other industries is so easily explained. If market imperfections are the root cause of regulation, then Posner, justifiably, suggests that one should find regulation imposed primarily in the highly concentrated industries, that is, those most likely

TABLE 2 Method of Valuation Generally Applied

Agency	The Method of Determining Rate Base Specifically Prescribed by			Section Number of Case Citation	Method Prescribed	Brief Explanation of Method
	Statute	Regulation	Court Decision			
FCC[a]					Original cost	Net original cost for test year
FERC			X		Original cost	Modified
Alabama PSC	X	X	X		Original cost	Original cost less depreciation
Alaska PC					Original cost	
Alaska PUC	X			A.S. 4205.441 81 (3)	Original cost	Cost of property when first devoted to public use or prudent acquistion cost
Alberta PUB	X				Original cost	
Arizona CC			X	80 Ariz. 145	Fair value	RCN determined by either trending or pricing; depreciation determined by age, life ratio
Arkansas PSC	X	X	X		Original cost	Depreciated original cost
California PUC					Original cost	
Colorado PUC		X			Original cost	
Connecticut PUCA					Original cost	
Delaware PSC	X			26 Del. Code	Original cost	
D.C. PSC	X			D.C. Code, Title 43 et seq.	Original cost	Depreciated original cost
Florida PSC	X			366.06 electric and gas 364.03 telephone 367.081 water and sewer	Prudent investment / Other / Prudent investment	Prudent investment for electric and gas; the telephone statute requires only that the rates be fair, just, reasonable, and sufficient; for all practical purposes, the commission employs original cost; for water and sewer, a fair return on the utility's investment in property.
Georgia PSC		X			Original cost	

TABLE 2 Method of Valuation Generally Applied (*Cont.*)

Agency	The Method of Determining Rate Base Specifically Prescribed by			Section Number of Case Citation	Method Prescribed	Brief Explanation of Method
	Statute	Regulation	Court Decision			
Hawaii PUC		X[e]	X	D. 1167 Hawaii Electric C.	Original cost	
Idaho PUC			X		Original cost	
Illinois CC					Original cost	
Indiana PSC	X			I.C. 8-1-2-6	Fair value	
Iowa SCC				U-138, Davenport Water Company	Original cost	Net investment rate base with cost of capital
Kansas SCC		X	X	192 Kans. 39	Original cost	
Kentucky PSC	X		X		Original cost Reproduction cost Prudent investment Other	Capital structure and other element of value recognized by law
Louisiana PSC		X	X		Original cost	Original cost
Maine PUC	X				Original cost	Original cost plus prudent acquisition cost, other also if relevant
Maryland PSU	X				Fair value	Evidence of current value based on TOC, CPI, IPI, reproduction cost, or appraisal considered
Massachusetts DPU		X			Original cost	
Michigan PSC	X[d]	X	X		Original cost Prudent investment	If plant carried is imprudent investment, we do not include that investment in original cost rate base; Electric statute specifies fair value, cost, etc., to be considered; gas and telephone statutes do not specify
Minnesota PSC	X	X		M.S. 237.08, telephone only	Original cost	Original cost prescribed by statute; as to electric and gas, the PSC decision, in the

Commission				Legal citation	Basis	Notes
Mississippi PSC			X	M.S., Ch. 216B, Sec. 16, Subd. 6, electric and gas only	Fair value	Northern States Power company preceeding, dated 6/2/75, stated that the PSC will not accept testimony on fair value or current value in any utility rate case, but will insist on original cost data for rate base purposes
Missouri PSC	X			308SW 2nd 704, 532SW 2nd 20	Fair value	In arriving at fair value, original cost, reproduction cost, and prudent investment would all be considered
Montana PSC	X			Tobacco River Power vs. MRRC	Fair value	Consider original cost and trended original cost and other relevant factors
Nebraska PSC[a]				75-609	Other	Determined by trending Handy Whitman index used by most companies; depreciation reserve has been trended
Nevada PSC	X				Original cost	Must consider current value; most use trended investment
New Hampshire PUC		X			Original cost	
New Jersey BPUC	X			Sup. Ct. in re *Sand Rates Case*, 66, No. 12 (1974)	Other	No particular method or combination of methods; board must consider all evidence submitted
New Mexico PSC	X			68-S-14 NMSA, 1953	Fair value	No State Supreme Court decision except with general statement of "fair value"; several district court decisions; must consider history and development of the property and business, original cost, reproduction cost as going concern and other elements recognized by laws of land
New Mexico SCC[a]					Original cost less depreciation	
New York PSC					Original cost	
North Carolina UC	X				Fair value	In addition to the use of trending and various indices, the commission may and does combine any and all other factors it deems

TABLE 2 Method of Valuation Generally Applied (*Cont.*)

| Agency | The Method of Determining Rate Base Specifically Prescribed by | | | Section Number of Case Citation | Method Prescribed | Brief Explanation of Method |
	Statute	Regulation	Court Decision			
						relevant to the final fair value determination; the statute provides this wide discretion by the commission; the book depreciation ratio is maintained in the final fair value determination
North Dakota PSC	X		X	49-02-03, NDCC	Prudent investment	Amount invested by utility, any excess over original cost allowed in rate basis if approved by the commission
Ohio PUC	X			4909.05, R.C.	Original cost	
Oklahoma CC	X			Title 17, Sec. 137, Laws 1959, p. 86, Sec. 3	Fair value	Fair return on fair value—telephone companies only; All other—depreciated original cost
Ontario EB	X			R.S.O.1970, C-312, S.19	Prudent investment	
Ontario TSC	X			Section 12	Original cost	
Oregon PUC					Original cost	No specific statutory provision
Pennsylvania PUC	X	X			Fair value	The fair value approach utilized by this commission gives weight to original cost, trended original cost, and/or depreciation reserve requirement is utilized for rate making
Puerto Rico PSC	X				Original cost	
Quebec PSB and EGB	X		X		Original cost	
Rhode Island PUC			X		Original cost	
South Carolina PSC		X			Original cost	Original cost less depreciation

Commission			Statute	Standard	Description
South Dakota PUC	X		SDCL49-34A-19	Original cost	
Tennessee PSC	X			Original cost	Original cost of property used and useful—financed by debt and equity investors
Texas PUC	X			Fair value	Original cost less depreciation and current cost less an adjustment for age and condition
Texas RC[b]	X		*Railroad Commission of Texas vs. Houston Natural Gas Corp.*, 289 S.W. 2nd 559 (Tex. 1956)	Fair value	For description of method used, see the Texas Public Utility Regulatory Act of 1975, Sections 39, 40, 41; Tex. Rev. Civ. Stat. Ann. Art. 1446c (Supp. 1976); rate base method is currently under litigation
Utah PSC				Original cost	Original cost and prudent investment
Vermont PSB	X			Original cost	Net investment in property prudently acquired for and devoted to public use.
Virgin Islands PSC[c]	X	X	30 V.I.C. 23	Fair value	
Virginia SCC		X		Net original cost	
Washington UTC	X		19 Wn. (2nd) 200, (1943)	Other	Any method or combination of methods warranted by law
West Virginia PSC				Original cost	
Wisconsin PSC		X		Other	Original cost of utility plant used and useful in providing service
Wyoming PSC	X			Original cost	Year end data used

[a] No commission regulation of electric or gas utilities—telephone only.

[b] No commission regulation of electric or telephone utilities.

[c] Electric facilities are government owned and operated but are regulated by the PSC for changes in rates. No gas service in the Virgin Islands other than bottle gas which is not regulated by the PSC.

[d] Electric statute specifies fair value, cost, etc., to be considered. Gas and telephone statutes do not specify.

[e] Based on commission decision.

TABLE 3 Items Allowed in Rate Base

The Agency Allows the Following in Rate Base

Agency	Land Held for Future Use	Property Held for Future Use	Construction Work in Progress	Allowance for Funds Used During Construction [21]	Contributions in Aid of Construction—Credit	Advance Payments	Research and Development	An Inflation Factor	Excess of Cost over Original Cost	Materials and Supplies	Allowance for Working Capital	Customer Advances—Credit	Accumulated Tax Deferrals—Credit	Pollution Control Equipment
FCC [53,54]	X[1]	X[1]	X[76]							X	X			X
FERC	X	X		X		X	X			X	X	X	[62]	X
Alabama PSC		X	X	X						X	X			X
Alaska PC [70]		X	X	X			X			X	X			
Alaska PUC	X[2]	X[2]		X	[26]					X	X	X	X	X
Alberta PMC						[42]				X[69]	X[30]		X	X
Alberta PUB [68]				[15]	X					X	X		X	X
Arizona CC	X[2]	X	[15]		X	X	X	[37]		X	X	X	X	X
Arkansas PSC	X[2]		X[16]	X[71]	X	X	X		X[39]	X	X	X	X	X
California PUC	X[3]			X	X	X	X			X	X[47]	X	X	X
Colorado PUC	X[3]	X[3]	X[17]	X	X	X				X	X	X	X	X
Connecticut PUCA					X			X		X	X		X	X
Delaware PSC	X	X	X[72]	X[73]	X		X			X	X	X	X	X
D.C. PSC	X	X	X[22]	X[67]	X					X[72]	X	X	X[51]	X
Florida PSC	X[4]	X		X	[66]		X[33]		X[40]	X	X		X	X
Georgia PSC	X[4]	X[4]	X		X		X			X	X	X	X	X
Hawaii PUC	X[4]	X[4]		X	X					X	X		X	X
Idaho PUC	X[6]	X[6]		X						X	X			X

	1	2	3	4	5	6	7	8	9	10	11	12	13	14	15	16	17	18
Illinois CC	X[7]	X[7]	X[7]	X[19]	X[29]	X[27]	X	X			X[48]	X	X	X	X	X	X	X
Indiana PSC	X[7]	X[7]	X	X	X	X	X				X	X	X	X	X	X	X	X
Iowa SCC	X[8]	[9]	[20]	X	X						X	X	X	X	X	X		X
Kansas SCC	[9]				X	X					X	X	X	X	X	X		
Kentucky PSC	X	X	X	X[27]	X	X[27]			X		X	X	X	X	X	X[27]	X[27]	X
Louisiana PSC	X	X	X[4]	X[27]	X	X[27]			X[41]		X	X	X	X	X	X[27]	X[27]	X
Maine PUC	X	X[10]	X	X	X	X		X	X[41]		X	X	X	X	X	X	X	X
Maryland PSC	X[10]	X[10]	X	X	X	X[31]	X[35]			X[49]	X	X	X	X	X	X	X	X
Massachusetts DPU	X[44]		X	X	X[27]	X	X			[49]	X[46]	X	X	X	X	X	X	X
Michigan PSC	X	X	X[74]	X[74]	[74]	X	[34]				X	X	X	[34]				
Minnesota PSC	X	X	X[74]		X	X		X[43]		[34]	X	X	X	X	X	X	X	X
Mississippi PSC	X	X	X	X	X	X					X	X	X	X	X	X	X	X
Missouri PSC	X	X		X	X	X	X	X			X	X	X	X	X	X	X	X
Montana PSC				X	X	X				X	X	X	X	X	X	X	X	X
Nebraska PSC[54]	[11]	[11]		X	X	X		X			X	X	X[11]	X	X	X	X	X
Nevada PSC	X[12]	X[12]		X	X	[32]	X[35]		X		X	X	X	X	X	X[52]	[11]	X
New Hampshire PUC	X[12]	X[12]	X[22]	X	X			X	X		X	X	X	X	X	X[52]	X[22]	X
New Jersey BPU	X		X[23]	[22]	[22]		X[75]	X			X	X	X	X	X	X		X
New Mexico PSC		X	X	X	X	X		X			X	X	X	X	X	X		
New Mexico SCC		X	X	X	X	X					X	X	X	X	X	X		
New York PSC	X	X	X	X	X			[36]			X	X	X	X	X	X[51]	X[51]	X
North Carolina UC		X	X	X	X	X			X		X	X	X	X	X	X		
North Dakota PSC		X	X	X	X	X					X	X	X	X	X	X	X	X
Ohio PUC	X	X[63]	[18]	X	X	X	X				X	X	X	X	X	X	X	X
Oklahoma CC	X	X	[64]	X	X	X[75]	X[75]				X	X	X	X	X	X	X	X
Ontario EB			[5]	X	X	X					X	X	X	X	X	X		X
Ontario TSC			X	X	X	X					X	X	X	X	X	X		
Oregon PUC	X[13]	X[13]	[57]	X	X	X		[57]			X	X	X	X	X	X[50]	X[50]	X
Pennsylvania PUC	X	X	X[25]	X	X	X		X			X	X	X	X	X	X	X	X
Puerto Rico PSC				X							X	X	X		X			
Quebec PSB and EGB			X	X	X	X					X	X	X	X	X	X	X	X
Rhode Island PUC	X	X[10]		X	X	X		X[55]			X	X	X	X	X	X[55]	X	X
South Carolina PSC				X	X	X	X				X	X	X	X	X	X	X	X
South Dakota PUC			X	X	X	X	X	X			X	X	X	X	X	X	X	X

TABLE 3 Items Allowed in Rate Base (Cont.)

The Agency Allows the Following in Rate Base

Agency	Land Held for Future Use	Property Held for Future Use	Construction Work in Progress	Allowance for Funds Used During Construction[21]	Contributions in Aid of Construction—Credit	Advance Payments	Research and Development	An Inflation Factor	Excess of Cost over Original Cost	Materials and Supplies	Allowance for Working Capital	Customer Advances—Credit	Accumulated Tax Deferrals—Credit	Pollution Control Equipment
Tennessee PSC	X	X	X[58]	X	X				X[44]	X	X	X	X	X
Texas PUC	X	X	X		X	X		X		X	X		X	X
Texas RC[56]	X	X	X	X	X		X	X	X	X	X	X	X	X
Utah PSC	X	X	X[24]	X						X	X			X
Vermont PSB	X	X		X		X	X			X	X			X
Virgin Islands PSC	X	X					X[33]				X			X
Virginia SCC	X	X	X	X		X	X			X	X		X	X
Washington UTC	X	X	65	X[38]	X[27]	X			X[45]			X	X	X
West Virginia PSC	X	X	28		X	X				X	X	X	X	X
Wisconsin PSC	59	59	14		X					X		X	61	X
Wyoming PSC			X	X	X[60]					X	X	X		X

[1] For gas utilities, to a limited extent. For electric utilities; "yes" for land and "no" for property held for future use.

[2] Discretionary.

[3] If to be used in not too distant future.

[4] Must meet tests of reasonableness.

[5] Construction work in progress normally disallowed. If included, AFDC on such assets is included in utility income.

[6] In certain instances depending on plan for use in immediate future.

7 Where planned use is known and it will be used in a reasonable period of time.

8 Current policy is to allow land held for future use in rate base only if it is part of a definite short-range construction plan.

9 Land and property held for future use are not always allowed, especially if no definite plan for the use is in sight.

10 If definite plan in foreseeable future.

11 Conditional.

12 If held for a definite purpose.

13 When the land or property will be used in the reasonably near future.

14 Although construction work in progress is not directly included in rate base, the rate of return on net investment rate base is adjusted so that in effect construction work in progress is included in net investment rate base up to an amount equal to 10% of rate base.

15 Either CWIP or interest charged to construction is allowed, not both.

16 Completed but not interest bearing.

17 Electric and gas—no; Telephone—yes.

18 Includable in rate base at discretion of commission if 75% complete on date certain and allowance for CWIP does not exceed 20% of total valuation.

19 Decided on a case-by-case basis considering in-service dates and cash flow requirements among other factors.

20 Construction work in progress on which AFUDC has not been capitalized has been included in rate base in some rate case proceedings.

21 AFUDC as an account balance does not appear directly in the rate base. Rate base effect takes place at that time when property to which AFUDC is related is allowed in rate base.

22 Based on facts and circumstances on the case in question.

23 Allowed only if interest has not been capitalized.

24 Interest-bearing CWIP is excluded from rate base.

25 Primarily, nonrevenue producing.

26 Deduct unamortized CIAC relating to depreciable contributed plant.

27 These items are used to reduce rate base.

28 Complete and in service.

29 Only interest charged to construction already capitalized to plant in service; depreciation on same allowed in cost of service; book-tax timing differences flowed through to the income statement.

30 Includes stored gas and capitalized permit costs.

31 If proper and necessary.

32 Usually.

TABLE 3 Items Allowed in Rate Base (Cont.)

[33] On those projects which are successfully completed and capitalized; unsuccessful projects expensed or accumulated and amortized.

[34] Not considered.

[35] Reasonable amount.

[36] General R &D is allowed as an operating expense—R&D performed in connection with a specific project would, of course, become part of rate base if such project ultimately became part of plant in service.

[37] Not specific.

[38] For major electric generation and related transmission expenditures.

[39] Plant acquisition adjustment if beneficial to customers.

[40] Prudent acquisition adjustments are sometimes permitted in rate base and amortization thereof in cost of service.

[41] Original cost plus prudent acquisition cost.

[42] Carrying costs for eligible advance payments and take or pay payments are expensed monthly rather than included in rate base.

[43] If utility is resold to a new company and price of items of plant accounts are reasonable. Otherwise, excessive cost would be charged to surplus over future years.

[44] Under some circumstances.

[45] Only if commensurate benefit to the rate payer is shown.

[46] Less appliances.

[47] With offset of accrued property taxes.

[48] If not offset by other cash flows.

[49] Only if justified—not allowed in all cases.

[50] When not included as interest- and dividend-free capital.

[51] But used as cost-free capital.

[52] When required or needed by state or federal agency.

[53] Net book cost of plant in service, property held for future use, construction work in progress (projects with expected completion dates under 1 year receive rate base treatment; those with expected completion dates greater than 1 year receive an allowance for funds used during construction—Docket 19129, plus materials and supplies actually paid for plus allowance for cash working capital. Customer advances are used as a credit to reduce the rate base; accumulated tax deferrals are used as a credit reducing the rate base.

[54] No commission regulation of electric or gas utilities.

[55] Not yet tested before the PUC.

[56] No commission regulation of electric or telephone utilities.

[57] For electric—yes, with AFDC included in income. All others, interest bearing CWIP is excluded from rate base.

[58] If interest charged to construction is included in income.

[59] If supported by impending usefulness for utility service.

[60] Deduct from rate base.

[61] Deduct from rate base in some cases; not where gas utilities are participating in gas exploration within the state.

[62] Account 281 included in capitalization for rate of return at zero cost.

[63] If use is imminent in the very near future.

[64] 1975 ruling on a case-by-case basis with certain restrictions.

[65] In extraordinary circumstances; then only production facilities and related transmission with AFUDC included as operating income.

[66] Used to reduce rate base for water and sewer utilities.

[67] Only interest charged on construction already closed to plant in service; depreciation on same allowed in cost of services.

[68] Statute prescribes the determination of rate base "for property of the owner that is used or required to be used in his service to the public within Alberta."

[69] Included in working capital.

[70] Methodology still being refined.

[71] Capitalized upon completion.

[72] 13-month average for electric, not telephone and gas.

[73] For telephone and gas, not electric.

[74] Minnesota Statute Sec. 216b.16, Sub 6a provides in part that the commission shall determine in its descretion whether and to what extent the income used in determining the actual return on the utility property shall include an allowance for funds used during construction based on magnitude, impact on cash flow, benefit to customers, and whether it will be immediately useful.

[75] For insurance, etc., but excludes advances for exploration and drilling for new sources of supply for natural gas.

[76] Limited to expenditures for pollution control and for oil- or natural-gas-fueled plants to use as other fuels.

to exert monopolistic policies. Posner [44] reports that, in general, this is simply not the case:

> Few, if any, responsible students of the airline industry, for example, believe that there is some intrinsic peculiarity about the market for air transportation that requires prices and entry to be fixed by the government. The same may be said for trucking, taxi service, stock brokerages, ocean shipping. . . .

An alternative theory of governmental regulation has been coined the *capture theory*. This theory holds that regulation has nothing to do with public interest; rather regulation is a process in which various interest groups vie for control. Posner summarizes the theory in the following syllogism:

> Big business—the capitalists—control the institutions of our society. Among those institutions is regulation. The capitalists must therefore control regulation.

The capture theory must be, in part, discounted since a large portion of regulation has nothing to do with big business. Farmers, truckers, barbers, union members, and many others are not in any manner connected with big business. The public interest theory seems to weaken when the wide spectrum of regulated activities is considered. But since there are examples in support of these theories, there may be some unification of the two that permits a more uniform understanding of the evolution of regulation. Such a theory can characterize a recent work of Stigler [54]. In his paper he hypothesized that regulation is but a product that is subject to the laws of supply and demand. In this framework, the product would be supplied to those who value it most highly. Apparently, the group who values it most highly could be either the public at large or other effective interest groups. In this manner a conciliation of both the public interest and capture theory can be realized.

ECONOMIC PRINCIPLES OF RATE REGULATION

Given that regulatory commissions act in the public interest, there is a set of economic criteria for them to follow. Lerner [32] points out that there are two basic functions of the price mechanism: discouraging the buyer from consuming too much and inducing the supplier to produce enough. The ideal output is one in which the marginal social benefit is equal to marginal social cost, a situation which is automatic in the perfectly competitive economy without externalities. In something less than this ideal case, the Pareto optimal solution of equating marginal benefits with marginal social costs may not be obtained. The monopolistic nature of the typical public utility is the standard example where the ideal functioning of the role of price may be disturbed.

Lerner [32] defines a public utility in a pragmatic manner:

When government is sufficiently concerned about the excessiveness of price charged for a commodity to feel it must correct this, even though price regulation would be required, we have a public utility and the problem of how prices should be regulated.

A common cliche characterizing the role of price regulation is as a *substitute for competition*. Lerner cautions, though, that this simplistic explanation can be misleading:

> . . . there is a danger of coming to regard perfect competition as an end in itself, rather than as one way in which marginal social benefit may be brought into equality with marginal social cost so that the price mechanism can carry out its basic social functions.

With perfect competition and no externalities four quantities determined by the production strategy of a firm are all equal (in the long run):

- Price
- Marginal revenue
- Average cost
- Marginal cost

Lerner suggests that one might consider the feasibility of prescribing a regulatory structure based on equating any two of these quantities. Since there are four quantities, one needs to consider six alternatives, that is, choose all possible pairs. This is done as follows:

1. *Price = Marginal Revenue*
The relation cannot be imposed, since it is just a description of the role of price in a perfectly competitive state of the market.

2. *Marginal Revenue = Marginal Cost*
This relation need not be imposed: Such a state is automatically reached by a profit-maximizing firm. However, since externalities are not included, marginal social revenue does not equal marginal social cost.

3. *Marginal Cost = Average Cost*
This state could possibly be imposed by regulators, and it sounds like a reasonable idea since this relationship holds when average cost is at a minimum. But what is really needed is something completely different. The *right* output should be produced at minimum average cost.

4. *Price = Average Cost*
This is price regulation as we know it today. This equality is illustrated via the following relationship (see Olsen [40]):

$$RR = E + d + T + (V - D)s$$

where RR = revenue requirement
       E = operating expenses
       d = annual depreciation
       T = taxes
       V = gross valuation of property
       D = accrued depreciation
       s = rate of return

Based on historical experience, sometimes a representative and recent 12-month period, the rate s is set so that the revenue requirement of the utility is satisfied. One of the chief objectives of the process is to determine a revenue requirement that will allow the firm to attract and maintain an appropriate capital base.

In its simplest form, the revenue received by the utility will be $\overline{p}\overline{q}$, where $\overline{q}$ is the quantity sold at the average price $\overline{p}$. Although this is highly simplified in that the utility may have several customer classes that are levied fees based on other than simply energy used, it is clear that the average price

$$\overline{p} = \frac{E + d + T + (V - D)s}{\overline{q}}$$

will suffice to cover all costs including a rate of return of s on the net asset base.

5. Price = Marginal Cost

This relationship is the one in which the socially optimal goal of equating value and marginal cost is obtained, one in which resources are allocated in an efficient manner. It is this relationship that is at the root of studies related to peak load pricing experiments for various electric utilities.

6. Average Cost = Marginal Revenue

This criterion is the converse of relation 5. That is, it may be applied to monopsonists, controlling their input prices as buyers. As monopsony is rare, this criterion is little discussed.

Since it is generally agreed (at least by economists) that relation 5 achieves an efficient allocation of resources, why is it that relation 4 predominates rate regulation structures in present times? Part of the answer is that in past years the marginal cost of electricity has been below average cost. This results from utilities being natural monopolies and from technological change. A marginal cost policy in this period would have presented a special problem in that some type of government subsidy to the utility would have been required to maintain utility solvency. With price below average cost, insufficient revenues are provided to meet total costs. Since marginal (and average) costs in the electric utility industry were actually declining in the 1950s and early 1960s, there seemed little motivation on anyone's part to deviate from average cost policies. Consumers were happy to see falling prices, and regulatory lag increased the actual rates of return above those allowed by the state PUCs.

The present situation is much different. Marginal costs are higher than average costs in nominal dollars, and there seems to be some interest from all parties involved to at least test the desirability and feasibility of various time of day and seasonal pricing policies that are oriented toward a marginal cost pricing regime. For some utilities a seasonal pricing policy is already in effect. Such a seasonal policy has the virtue that its implementation is almost costless as compared to a full-scale metering system required for time of day, peak load pricing. Full-fledged marginal cost pricing is unlikely, however, because of the difficulties of measurement. Also, with the average costs below marginal costs, utilities would be able to retain the rents on existing equipment that currently are passed on to consumers under average cost pricing. This is politically unpalatable. Consequently, average cost pricing will most likely continue to be the dominant form of utility regulation.

There are many ways to implement an average cost pricing scheme. The A-J view is that public utility commissions specify an average rate of return and allow utilities the opportunity to set their prices to achieve the allowed rate of return, which is above the cost of capital. This is the way American Telephone and Telegraph is regulated by the Federal Communications Commission. Alternatively, public utility commissions may specify prices and allow utilities to maximize profits. Prices are raised when the returns are insufficient and lowered when the returns are too high. As long as the target rate of return is above the cost of capital, this approach to regulation has consequences similar to the A-J view, although there are some differences. See Burness et al. [12] for a discussion of this. If the target rate of return is the cost of capital, then according to the A-J model, utility behavior is indeterminant. (If subsidiary objectives are added, the model becomes determinant. For example, if incentives are specified that lead to a desire to maximize kilowatt-hour sales, costs are minimized.)

A third view is presented by Joskow [29]. He proposes that public utility commissions are mainly interested in not raising rates to customers. Therefore, when costs are declining, there are no efforts to lower rates beyond reductions desired by the utility, and rates of return are allowed to rise. In inflationary periods, the public utility commissions delay rate increases as long as possible and allow fuel adjustment clauses to shift the burden of higher prices to other institutions. How utility decisions should be modeled under this regime needs further exploration. An obvious conclusion is that there is a strong incentive to keep costs not covered by automatic pass-throughs from rising.

In conclusion, there is no clear opinion as to how to represent the interactions of regulatory commissions and the utilities they regulate. In Chapter 3 we shall describe the A-J theory in detail. In Chapter 4 we shall present the empirical evidence resulting from tests of the A-J hypothesis.

3

THE AVERCH-JOHNSON THESIS

REVIEW OF THE MAIN RESULTS

Averch and Johnson (A-J) [2] published their landmark paper dealing with monopolies subject to regulation in 1962. Their conjecture and methods still embody a widely accepted interpretation of the behavior of a monopoly under regulation. Certain extensions and clarifications of the A-J thesis have been published by Wellisz [59], Takayama [56], Baumol and Klevorick [8], Zajac [64], Bailey and Malone [6], and Jaffee [27] as well as many others.

A-J consider a monopoly with a production function given by $q = F(x_1, x_2)$ in which

$$x_1 = \text{capital stock}$$

$$x_2 = \text{labor}$$

with factor costs r_1 and r_2, respectively. Denote by $p(q)$ the inverse demand function. The profit-maximizing firm would seek a quantity q which maximizes

$$\max f(x_1, x_2) = p(q)q - r_1 x_1 - r_2 x_2 \tag{1}$$

The objective in (1) is for the unregulated firm. The intersection of the marginal revenue curve with the marginal cost curve is obtained by setting $\partial f / \partial x_i = 0$, $i = 1, 2$; that is,

$$qp'(q) \frac{\partial F}{\partial x_i} + p(q) \frac{\partial F}{\partial x_i} - r_i = 0 \tag{2}$$

Rewriting (2) provides

$$[qp'(q) + p(q)] \frac{\partial F}{\partial x_i} = r_i \qquad (3)$$

Relation (3) shows for the unregulated firm buying its factors of production in perfect markets that

$$\frac{\partial F / \partial x_1}{\partial F / \partial x_2} = \frac{r_1}{r_2} \qquad (4)$$

That is, the ratio of the marginal products is equal to the ratio of factor prices. This is called the *marginal rate of technical substitution*.

The situation investigated by A-J is the case in which profits are regulated by some external government commission; that is, a constraint on profits is appended to the objective function in (1). Suppose that profit is upper-bounded by some fixed percentage of total capital investment; for example, consider the constraint

$$\frac{p(q)q - r_2 x_2}{x_1} \leq s \qquad (5)$$

Assuming the initial capital stock is zero, inequality (5) states that total revenue less labor costs per dollar of capital cannot exceed some prescribed allowed return of $s\%$. In other words, if the firm invests \$100 in capital while $s = .15$, then the firm's revenues less expenses cannot exceed \$15. Constraint (5) then makes sense only if the cost of capital $r_1 < s$. Otherwise, the firm would lose money. The behavior of the monopoly is explored by A-J through analyzing the solutions and characteristics of the following optimization problem:

$$\text{Max } p(q)q - r_1 x_1 - r_2 x_2$$
$$\text{s.t. } p(q)q - sx_1 - r_2 x_2 \leq 0 \qquad (6)$$
$$q = F(x_1, x_2)$$
$$x_1, x_2 \geq 0$$

The basic conjecture of A-J is that, in general, an optimal solution of (6) provides inputs (x_1^*, x_2^*) that do not satisfy (4). This can be seen directly by noting that if (5) is binding in (6), the solution to (4) is infeasible. There is a specific bias that results. The A-J thesis is as follows: For any given output level, say q_2 in Figure 6, the firm will tend to invest more capital and less labor than the cost minimization solution. The dashed lines in Figure 6 represent the family of straight lines $r_1 x_1 + r_2 x_2$, so that the heavy dots represent the efficient production path. The nature of the A-J solution is illustrated by the point x on curve q_2.

Zajac [81] provides an illuminating geometric argument for the reason that the optimal solution to (6) has a capital bias. The analysis starts with Figure 6 in which the production frontiers of three output levels are shown. Assume that $p(q)q$ is concave; the isoprofit lines of $p(q)q - r_1 x_1 - r_2 x_2$ in the (x_1, x_2) plane would be as shown in Figure 7. The unconstrained maximum in Figure 7 is not, in

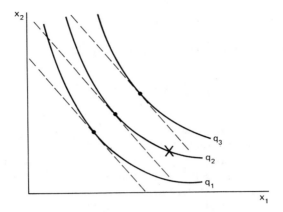

Figure 6   Efficient input combinations.

general, feasible for (6) due to the rate-of-return constraint. By adding an extra coordinate to the problem and setting P equal to profit, $P = p(q)q - r_1x_1 - r_2x_2$, the regulatory constraint in (6) becomes

$$P - (s_1 - r_1)x_1 \leq 0 \tag{7}$$

That is, the regulatory constraint now is a hyperplane that contains the x_2 axis. The projection onto the (x_1, x_2) plane of the intersection of (7) with the profit function is shown in Figure 8.

The shaded region in Figure 8 represents input combinations (x_1, x_2) that *do not* satisfy the regulatory constraint; that is, these are inputs which result in a higher profit than the regulatory constraint permits. A superpositioning of Figure 6 onto Figure 8 is illustrated in Figure 9.

It is assumed that the unconstrained maximum in Figure 6 lies in the interior of the "teardrop." Two alternative production expansion paths are shown in Figure 9. The production path $O\text{-}P$, shown in heavy dots, is the cost-minimizing path.

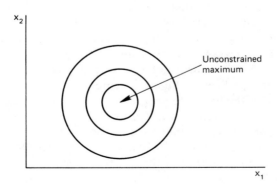

Figure 7   Iso-profit lines.

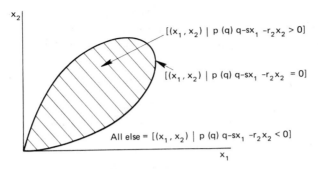

Figure 8   Regulatory constraint.

Path $O\text{-}P'$ is another production path using a larger proportion of x_1. Points A and A' represent two alternatives for producing the same quantity of output. Given that $O\text{-}P$ is the least cost production path, let A be the profit-maximizing point, that is, the solution to (1). Zajac argues as follows:

Hypothesis.   If the efficient production path is $O\text{-}P$, then point B characterizes the solution of (6).

Implication.   At output level q^* the unconstrained firm would use less capital and more labor.

Proof of Hypothesis (*Geometric*). Suppose that B lies above the cost-minimizing path; that is, let the efficient production path be $O\text{-}P'$, and let A' be the unconstrained optimum to (1). In this case point C would be more profitable than B; furthermore, due to the concavity of the profit function, point D would be even more attractive. But point D is feasible, which would contradict the optimality of point B. The conclusion is that B must lie below (or on) the efficient locus of points $O\text{-}P$.

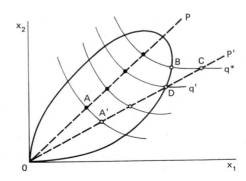

Figure 9   Profit maximization under regulation.

A rigorous analysis of this behavior was first done by A-J [3] using the Kuhn-Tucker *necessary* conditions for an optimal solution to (6). A-J show that these necessary conditions imply that for an optimal (x_1^*, x_2^*) the following is true:

$$\frac{\partial F / \partial x_1}{\partial F / \partial x_2} = \frac{r_1}{r_2} - \frac{\lambda^*(s - r_1)}{(1 - \lambda^*)r_2} \tag{8}$$

where λ^* is an optimal Kuhn-Tucker vector (in this case a scalar). If $0 < \lambda^* < 1$ and $s > r_1$, then

$$\frac{\partial F / \partial x_1}{\partial F / \partial x_2} < \frac{r_1}{r_2} \tag{9}$$

which is the algebraic equivalent of the firm choosing an inefficient combination of capital and labor; that is, $\partial F / \partial x_1$, the marginal product of capital, is proportionately less than labor's marginal product. The dual variable λ^* may be interpreted as the fraction of increased revenue or decreased cost that must go into capital expenditures.

In 1970 Baumol and Klevorick [8] provided, under certain hypotheses, a satisfactory proof that $0 < \lambda^* < 1$. The following lemma is proved in [8]:

Lemma. If the firm maximizes its total profit subject to the regulatory constraint, that is, (6), and if, in addition, the constraint is binding and $x_1^* > 0$, $x_2^* > 0$, then $0 < \lambda^* < 1$.

The original conjecture by A-J [3] was that (8) implied the firm would overcapitalize. That is, from (8) it was asserted that x_1^* would be larger than the choice of capital for the unconstrained, profit-maximizing monopolist. Baumol and Klevorick [8] show that it is not necessarily true, however. A correct interpretation is given by Baumol and Klevorick [8]. This interpretation includes the following two highlights:

Fact 1. The firm described by (6) will, in general, adopt input proportions different from those which minimize the cost of the final output q^*.

Fact 2. The capital-labor ratio of the regulated firm will be larger than the one that minimizes costs for the given output level that it elects to produce. But the output level will certainly be different. If there is less output, there can be less capital, rather than more, used by the regulated firm.

Hence, the usual interpretation of A-J, that rate regulation causes the firm to *overcapitalize*, is true only in a specific context. Another erroneous conclusion reached by A-J [3] is that rate regulation necessarily causes the regulated firm to produce an output necessarily larger than one which maximizes profits. This conclusion was probably reached by noting that if overcapitalization occurred, then a larger output was inevitable. Baumol and Klevorick [8] give an example contradicting this notion as well as conditions for output to increase. An analysis of this conclusion leads Baumol and Klevorick [8] to the following summary:

> The invalidity of [a guaranteed larger output for the regulated firm] may perhaps be considered unfortunate. If it were true, it might have been claimed as a virtue of the regulatory process. For, generally, the monopolistic firm's output is taken to be smaller than the level that is socially optimal. . . . Indeed, some authors have defended fair rate of return regulation on grounds that it will have some beneficial effect on output. For example, Alfred E. Kahn [30] recognizes explicitly the input inefficiency such regulation can engender. But, he argues, by inducing the regulated firm to overinvest in capacity and hence to increase its output, fair rate of return helps to reduce—if not overcome—the monopoly's tendency to underinvest and restrict output. The fact that [a larger output] is not true as a general statement weakens somewhat the case of Kahn and others who take a similar position.

There are several other results and implications of the A-J model of regulation, (6), that have important ramifications:

1. Does the inefficiency of the regulated firm decrease as the allowed rate of return s approaches the cost of capital r_1?
2. Will the regulated firm ever *gold-plate*, that is, invest, in capital that is never used in productive output?

Baumol and Klevorick [8] show that, counter to one's intuition, as s approaches r_1 the use of capital actually increases. In particular, they show that

$$\frac{dx_1}{ds} < 0 \tag{10}$$

for $r_1 < s < r_m$, where r_m is the resulting rate of return on capital for the profit-maximizing (unconstrained) firm.

The implication of (10) in the regulatory setting is quite profound. It says that the closer the regulators can estimate the true cost of capital r_1, more, not less, capital inefficiency will result. Quoting from Baumol and Klevorick,

> . . . the result of better estimation of the cost of capital by the regulator may simply be to aggravate that inefficiency if the rise in the use of capital is not matched by an appropriate increase in the quantity of labor utilized.

GOLD PLATING AND OTHER FEATURES OF THE A-J SOLUTION

The notion of *gold plating* is that of a regulated firm adding completely nonproductive capital to its rate base. This type of inefficiency is much more blatant than the more subtle inefficiency of distorted capital-labor ratios. The question addressed in this section is whether gold plating can be, under certain circumstances, a result of rational behavior by a regulated firm.

One of the earliest studies of the gold-plating issue with an A-J framework is due to Zajac [64]. Zajac succeeded in characterizing the nature of gold-plating possibilities by considering a single-input version of the regulated firm. This simpler version uncomplicates the analysis and, also, permits a graphical explanation of gold-plating possibilities, laying the groundwork for the discussion of the A-J effect with Leontief production functions.

Although the nature of the production function used by Zajac was not formally specified, it is apparent that the model is as follows:

$$\text{Max } qp(q) - rx_1$$
$$qp(q) - sx_1 \leq 0$$
$$q \leq F(x_1) \tag{11}$$
$$q, x_1 \geq 0$$

where x_1, capital, is the sole input and $F(x_1)$ is the production function. In Zajac's analysis, $F(x_1)$ is simply x_1; hence, the relation $q \leq F(x_1)$ takes on the simple form $q \leq x_1$.

The next step seems trivial but is crucial. The inequality $q \leq x_1$ is replaced by an equality with the slack variable $\hat{K}$; that is,

$$q + \hat{K} = x_1 \tag{12}$$

$\hat{K}$ represents an amount of capital that enters the rate base but does not provide any output; that is, gold plating occurs if and only if $\hat{K} > 0$. Instead of explicitly including (12) in (11), Zajac substitutes directly for x_1. Moreover, he replaces q with K to emphasize that the output q is associated with useful capital, denoted by K. The model then becomes the following:

$$\text{Max } Kp(K) - rx_1$$
$$Kp(K) - sx_1 \leq 0$$
$$K + \hat{K} = x_1$$
$$\hat{K}, K, x_1 \geq 0$$

The substitution for x_1 yields the following:

$$\text{Max } R(K) - r(K + \hat{K})$$
$$R(K) - s(K + \hat{K}) \leq 0 \tag{13}$$
$$K, \hat{K} \geq 0$$

where $R(K)$ represents revenue and $R(K) = Kp(K)$.

With the model in (13), Zajac analyzes the gold-plating issue. The important aspect of this development is the manner in which the production function is integrated into the model. Note that the requirement $q = F(x_1)$ has been relaxed to $q \leq F(x_1)$. The slack variable $\hat{K}$ provides the relaxation in (13).

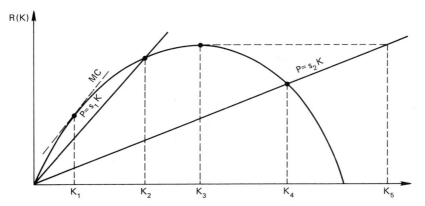

Figure 10   Revenue curves and regulation.

Consider Figure 10, where $P = P(K) = R(K) - rK$ represents net profit. The straight line $P = sK$ represents the regulatory bound on profit as a function of capital.

The five different values of K_i in Figure 10 are chosen to illustrate alternative conclusions about gold plating. First, if there is no regulation and the firm behaves as an ordinary profit-maximizing monopolist, then output is determined at the point where marginal cost (MC) is equal to marginal revenue. In Figure 10, this is the point K_1. Next, if profit is constrained by $P \leq s_1 K$, then output would increase to K_2. At point K_2, marginal revenue is still positive, and there is no motivation to pad the rate base. Point K_3 corresponds to an output at which marginal revenue is zero. If the allowed rate of return is decreased to $s_2 < s_1$, then it would appear that the firm should operate at K_4, a point where marginal revenue is negative. Here, profit would be $R(K_4) - rK_4$. But consider a rate-base-padding strategy. Capital K_3 is employed usefully, and a quantity $K_5 - K_3$ is acquired for padding only. The total profit in this alternative is $R(K_3) - rK_5$. Rate base padding is a rational response to regulation if

$$R(K_3) - rK_5 > R(K_4) - rK_4$$

or equivalently

$$R(K_3) - R(K_4) > r(K_5 - K_4)$$

Observe in Figure 10 that $s_2(K_5 - K_4) = R(K_3) - R(K_4)$. Since it is assumed that $s_2 > r$, the advantage of rate base padding is clear.

Hence, rate base padding (or gold plating) can be the rational response of a regulated firm that is modeled by (13). Moreover, it is no coincidence that gold plating possibilities (such as in Zajac's analysis) are derived in a framework for which the production function is specified by $q \leq F(x_1)$. This point is further clarified in the following numerical example:

$$p(q) = -q + 12$$

$$r = 3$$

$$s = 4$$

$$F(x_1) = x_1, \qquad \text{the production function}$$

The single-input A-J model, as specified by (11), is as follows:

$$\text{Max} -q^2 + 12q - 3x_1$$

$$-q^2 + 12q - 4x_1 \leq 0$$

$$q \leq x_1 \tag{14}$$

$$q, x_1 \geq 0$$

The optimal solution to (14) is $q^* = 6$, $x_1^* = 9$, which yields a net profit of 9. This solution specifies gold plating to the extent of $x_1^* - q^* = 3$. On the other hand, if the production function in (14) is specified as $q = x_1$, then another straightforward calculation provides $q^* = x_1 = 8$ with a net profit of 8. (The fact that the net profit could not be any larger in the case of equality is, of course, a foregone conclusion.)

At this point, the reader may wonder if gold plating possibilities depend, in part, on the form of the production function. Surprisingly, this is the case. The general result is simply the following:

Clearly, gold plating cannot occur in (6) if $q = F(x_1,x_2)$; that is, it is formally disallowed. Also gold plating *will not* occur in (6) for a large class of production functions $F(x_1,x_2)$ even when one allows $q \leq F(x_1,x_2)$. This is defined in Bailey's Proposition 5.3, described below.

This result seems to indicate a need for formally identifying two alternative interpretations of (6). Define *strong regulation* to be the model given by (6), that is, $q = F(x_1,x_2)$, and define *weak regulation* to be the model specified by (6) but with the important exception that $q \leq F(x_1,x_2)$. The notion of strong regulation is that the regulators not only control revenues but, in addition, ensure that $q = F(x_1,x_2)$, thereby eliminating (blatant) waste. In weak regulation, the latter behavior is not necessarily eliminated.

SOME WORK OF ELIZABETH BAILEY [5]

The notion that gold plating cannot occur under strong regulation is not a new one. This result, in an equivalent form, is given in Elizabeth Bailey's 1973 book on the A-J model [5].

Proposition 3.6 (Bailey)   . . . In the limiting case where all wasteful expense is excluded from the rate base, the profit maximizing firm never finds operation off the production frontier to be an optimal policy. . . .

One of the innovative features of Bailey's 1973 work [5] is that operation off the production frontier is explicitly modeled. Bailey's basic version of the A-J model is as follows:

$$\text{Max } R(x_1,x_2) - r_1(x_1 + \bar{x}_1) - r_2(x_2 + \bar{x}_2)$$

$$R(x_1,x_2) - s(x_1 + \bar{x}_1) - r_2(x_2 + \bar{x}_2) \leq 0 \quad (\lambda) \qquad (15)$$

$$x_1, \bar{x}_1, x_2, \bar{x}_2 \geq 0$$

where x_1, x_2 are useful capital and labor, $\bar{x}_1, \bar{x}_2$ are wasted capital and labor, and $R(x_1,x_2) = F(x_1,x_2)p[F(x_1,x_2)]$ is the revenue function and $F(x_1,x_2)$ is the production function. The variable λ is the Kuhn-Tucker variable associated with the regulatory constraint. Bailey [5] points out that the model (15) is essentially equivalent to the following:

$$\text{Max } R(q) - r_1x_1 - r_2x_2$$

$$R(q) - sx_1 - r_2x_2 \leq 0$$

$$q \leq F(x_1,x_2)$$

$$x_1,x_2 \geq 0$$

where $R(q) = qp(q)$ is the revenue function (see the footnote on page 73 of [5]).

Hence, (15) is simply another way of specifying the A-J model under *weak* regulation.

Bailey [5, Chap. 5] presents and proves a sequence of theorems that characterize the solution to the weakly regulated model of (15). These results so elegantly characterize the nature of (15) that they are repeated here. But before reviewing these results, it is important to emphasize that they do not necessarily apply to the strongly regulated case, the case which was implicitly assumed by most earlier writers, for example Averch and Johnson [3].

Proposition 5.1.   The Lagrange multiplier for (15) is bounded as follows: $0 \leq \lambda^* \leq r_1/s$.

Proposition 5.2.   The profit-maximizing firm constrained to earn no more than a fair return on its capital investment always finds it optimal to operate in a (strictly) elastic region of the revenue curve.

Proposition 5.3   The firm whose profits are limited to a fair return on capital investment will, if the marginal physical product of capital is positive, have no incentive to operate off the production frontier.

Proposition 5.4   The profit-maximizing firm, constrained to earn at most a fair return on investment, selects a production technique that uses a combination of more capital and less labor than is consistent with minimum cost operation.

Proposition 5.4 is the classical result of regulation based on rate of return; that is, an inefficient capital-labor ratio for the output level is chosen as long as the regulatory constraint is binding. Proposition 5.1 provides a tighter upper bound on λ^*, (r_1/s), than the original upper bound of 1. The two most interesting propositions are 5.2 and 5.3.

Proposition 5.2 is very fundamental. It states that under (weak) regulation the output level q^* must occur in the elastic portion of the revenue curve, that is, at a point where the price elasticity is greater than 1. The conclusion is obvious. Nevertheless, this result was highlighted by Bailey for the following reason:

> [A result] which has been virtually ignored in the literature. . . . Proposition 5.2 may prove useful in testing the appropriateness of the A-J model. If empirical results indicate that a firm is operating in the inelastic region of the revenue curve, then we can assert that the A-J model does not offer a valid explanation of the firm's behavior.

The point that Bailey emphasizes is that (under weak regulation) there is a consequence of higher order than inefficient capital-labor ratios. Proposition 5.2 shows that output levels of a regulated firm (acting in a rational fashion) never move into the inelastic region of demand. This is surprising since one usually associates regulated firms with goods which are price inelastic. The point Bailey makes is as follows. If the empirically measured price elasticity of a regulated firm is less than 1, the Proposition 5.2 shows that the behavior of the firm is not explained by the (weakly) regulated A-J model. This test, although much easier and more robust than any other, was not done by any of the authors surveyed for empirical evidence of the A-J thesis. The role of the demand elasticity is revisited in Chapter 6, since evidence suggests the elasticity is less than 1.

Proposition 5.2 is not necessarily true for a strongly regulated firm with a single-input production function. The numerical example (14) provides a counterexample. If the production function is specified as $q = x_1$, an optimal value of $q^* = 8$ is obtained. At $q^* = 8$, the marginal revenue is negative:

$$-2q + 12 \mid _{q=8} = -4$$

Hence, the price elasticity at $q^* = 8$ is less than 1. In addition, this example also illustrates another fundamental difference between weak and strong regulation. Proposition 5.1 is also not necessarily true under strong regulation. Since the optimal solution to (14) under strong regulation occurs at a point where the marginal revenue is negative, one can rewrite the equality constraint $q = x_1$ in the form $q \geq x_1$ and equality will still be obtained. Equivalently, the constraint can be written as $-q + x_1 \leq 0$ so that (14) becomes the following:

$$\text{Max } -q^2 + 12q - 3x_1$$

$$\text{s.t. } -q^2 + 12q - 4x_1 \leq 0 \qquad (\lambda)$$

$$-q \qquad + x_1 \quad \leq 0 \qquad (\mu)$$

$$q, x_1 \geq 0$$

With the constraints written as inequalities, both Kuhn-Tucker variables λ and μ are nonnegative. The Kuhn-Tucker necessary conditions provide

$$-2q + 12 = (-2q + 12)\lambda - \mu$$

$$-3 = -4\lambda + \mu$$

Since $q^* = 8$ is optimal, a straightforward calculation provides a solution $\lambda^* = 7/8$ and $\mu^* = 1/2$. In particular, note that $\lambda^* > r_1/s$, which shows that Proposition 5.1 is not necessarily valid under strong regulation.

By definition, gold plating cannot occur under strong regulation. Bailey's Proposition 5.3 shows that gold plating will not occur under weak regulation as long as the marginal product of (useful) capital is positive, that is, $\partial F/\partial x_1 > 0$. This result is a straightforward conclusion of the Kuhn-Tucker necessary conditions of (15). For the sake of completeness, Bailey's proof is given here.

Proof (*Proposition 5.3*). Suppose in (15) that $\bar{x}_1^* > 0$. From the Kuhn-Tucker conditions, it follows that $\lambda^* = r_1/s < 1$. Furthermore, by definition,

$$\frac{\partial R}{\partial x_1} = R' \frac{\partial F}{\partial x_1}$$

and the quantity is positive by virtue of Proposition 5.2 and the hypothesis. The Kuhn-Tucker conditions also imply (since $x_1^* > 0$)

$$\frac{\partial R}{\partial x_1} - r_1 = \lambda^* \frac{\partial R}{\partial x_1} - \lambda^* s$$

so that

$$(1 - \lambda^*) \frac{\partial R}{\partial x_1} = r_1 - \lambda^* s$$

Since $\lambda^* < 1$ and $\partial R/\partial x_1 > 0$, the left-hand side is positive. Hence, $r_1 - \lambda^* s > 0$, which implies $\lambda^* < r_1/s$ and a contradiction is obtained. Hence, $\bar{x}_1^* = 0$, and the proposition is proven.

It is Proposition 5.3 that apparently has dissuaded Bailey, and many other researchers, from pursuing the different notions of weak and strong regulation. The logic, which is entirely correct, depends, though, on the assumed form of the production function. In the proof of Proposition 5.3, two assumptions are used:

$$\text{(a)} \quad F(0,x_2) = F(x_1,0) = 0 \tag{16}$$

that is, some of each input is required, and

$$\text{(b)} \quad \frac{\partial F}{\partial x_1} > 0, \quad \frac{\partial F}{\partial x_2} > 0 \tag{17}$$

If these assumptions hold, then it is clear that $\partial F/\partial x_1$, the marginal physical product of capital, is positive at the optimal solution since it is positive everywhere. Hence, by Proposition 5.3 it follows that $\bar{x}_1$ and $\bar{x}_2$ can be eliminated from (15) without altering the solution; consequently, the case of weak regulation reduces to strong regulation. There is no apparent need for the different notion of weak regulation under the assumptions (16) and (17).

In most economic contexts, the assumptions (16) and (17) are not perceived, in general, as being excessively restrictive. In fact, the cumulative research and continuing discussion about the Averch-Johnson thesis does not seem to question this specification. Various empirical tests (discussed in Chapter 4) concerning the validity of the Averch-Johnson thesis have been based on different types of econometrically estimated, reduced-form production functions, for example, Cobb-Douglas. These production functions all have the common characteristic that output q is related to inputs, say capital, labor, and/or fuel, in some well-defined functional form. Each is a continuously differentiable function with parameters empirically estimated.

An alternative, engineering-based production function is one that includes an explicit representation of alternative technological processes. There may be a finite number of processes, say $a_1, a_2, \ldots, a_n$, and each process may require, per unit of output, a fixed amount of each input, for example, the Leontief input-output structure. The output of the production function is then determined by choosing relative intensities of the use of each process. The production function defined by a linear program is a variant of the latter type.

One important characteristic of the finitely generated, process-oriented production function is that it is not necessarily true that inputs can always be substituted for one another. Hence, it does not always follow that $\partial F/\partial x_i > 0$. Consequently, Proposition 5.3 may not be applicable.

EXTENSIONS TO PROCESS-ORIENTED PRODUCTION FUNCTIONS

In this section, the A-J model (6) is studied for the case in which the production function is based on a finite or restricted set of alternative production processes rather than a production function with continuously substitutable inputs for all x_1 and x_2. There is a question as to whether or not a finitely generated, or restricted, production function is not just an approximation to a continuous process and can be ignored.

For electric utilities the discussion is relevant because public utility commissions (PUCs) look at more than the rate of return. They have ready access to engineering estimates of costs for a given plant type and actual construction costs for all plants in the country. This allows them to exercise some control over the per kilowatt cost of a plant. Also, there is a relatively small set of technologies available to a utility. One can make a reasonable case that the finitely generated production function better represents utility options than one that is continuously differentiable. That is, in this context, strong regulation implies that regulatory commissions exercise judgment beyond just considerations of excessive additions of new capital. The PUCs are assumed to require a reasonable cost per kilowatt of a given plant type and maintain some control over the reserve margin.

Since $\partial F / \partial x_i = 0$ occurs with the process-oriented production function, Bailey's Proposition 5.3 is not applicable. Hence, in the weakly regulated case the firm may choose to operate off the production frontier. An important conclusion is that a significant difference exists between weak and strong regulation when the production function is defined by a finite set of technologically based processes or is restricted in some fashion.

Consider first an example of the continuously substitutable Cobb-Douglas production function:

$$F(x_1, x_2) = ax_1^\alpha x_2^\beta \tag{18}$$

Note that with a production function such as (18) any expansion path $(\overline{x_1}, \overline{x_2}) \in R_+^2$ (the nonnegative orthant) is possible. But suppose some of these paths are expressly eliminated due to technological constraints; for example, the nature of the technology or the regulatory commission may require

$$x_1 \leq 2x_2$$

The production function is now of a more complex form:

$$q = \begin{cases} F(x_1, x_2) & \text{if } x_1 \leq 2x_2 \\ F(2x_2, x_2) & \text{if } x_1 \geq 2x_2 \end{cases} \tag{19}$$

so that $\partial F / \partial x_i$ does not even exist along $x_1 - 2x_2 = 0$. Some typical isoquants of this production function illustrate how the substitutability of one factor for another becomes limited. See Figure 11. In particular, note that $\partial F / \partial x_1$ is zero in the region $x_1 > 2x_2$. Also note that Figure 11 depicts the isoquants under weak regulation. With strong regulation the region below the line $x_1 - 2x_2 = 0$ is expressly prohibited.

An illustration of the Leontief production function, one which possesses *corners*, is shown in Figure 12. In Figure 12, there are three different production processes, a_1, a_2, and a_3. A unit of output from each process a_i requires a fixed proportion of inputs, say (b_1^i, b_2^i). The production possibilities are defined by the following (polyhedral) convex set:

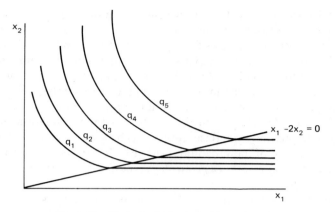

Figure 11   Limited substitution of factor inputs.

$$P = \{(q,x_1,x_2)|\ q = \sum_{i=1}^{3} \alpha_i, \alpha_i \geq 0, x_1 \geq \sum_{i=1}^{3} \alpha_i b_1^i,\ x_2 \geq \sum_{i=1}^{3} \alpha_i b_2^i\} \qquad (20)$$

The set P enters into the A-J model in the following manner:

$$\text{Max } qp(q) - r_1 x_1 - r_2 x_2$$

$$qp(q) - sx_1 - r_2 x_2 \leq 0 \qquad (21)$$

$$(q,x_1,x_2) \in P$$

Hence, the usual A-J model (under weak regulation) is the case in which

$$P = P_F = \{(q,x_1,x_2)|\ q \leq F(x_1,x_2)\} \qquad (22)$$

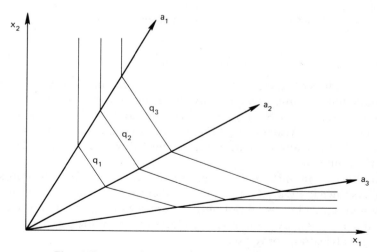

Figure 12   Isoquants with finitely many distinct processes.

where $F(x_1,x_2)$ is the assumed production function with $\partial F/\partial x_i$ existing and strictly greater than zero for $x_i \geq 0$, $i = 1, 2$.

The main difference between (20) and (22) is that in (20) there are regions for which marginal physical product of capital is zero, whereas in (22) there are not. Hence, the solution to (21) may involve gold plating, making a difference between weak and strong regulation in (21). Strong regulation corresponds to the case in which the constraints in (20) are modified so that

$$x_1 = \sum_{i=1}^{3} \alpha_i b_1^i, \qquad x_2 = \sum_{i=1}^{3} \alpha_i b_2^i$$

This means that productive inputs must necessarily lie within the convex set generated by rays a_1 and a_3 in Figure 12.

The fact that gold plating can occur when using a finitely generated production function (20) and cannot occur with a continuously substitutable production function (22) needs further explanation since the two models may be arbitrarily close approximations to one another. In Figure 13, two isoquants are drawn. Suppose that the dashed line is a polyhedral (approximation) to the continuously differentiable isoquant shown as the solid line. Let point B represent the optimal solution to the A-J model using the smooth production function $F(x_1,x_2)$. The amount of capital employed in this solution is $\bar{x}_1 + \hat{x}_1$. Next, let the dashed line represent a linear approximation to the isoquant $\bar{q} = F(x_1,x_2)$. For this polyhedral approximation, assume that the optimal solution is at point C (which should obviously be near B). But in this polyhedral approximation, a significant amount of gold plating $\hat{x}_1$ occurs. Hence, even though the optimal solutions are nearly identical, one solution is characterized by significant gold plating, while the other is not.

This observation means that gold plating is best viewed from a relative

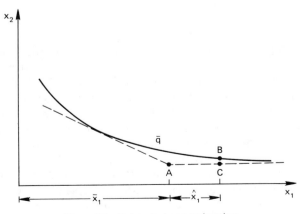

Figure 13 Polyhedral approximation.

point of view. Even though all the capital associated with the solution point C in Figure 13 is usefully employed, very little output is attributed to the portion labeled $\hat{x}_1$. The question is at what point should one conclude that the firm is "essentially" gold-plating?

In summary, the main point in this section is that certain classical results of the A-J model are derived in the special framework of fully substitutable production functions. For the case in which alternative expansion paths are limited, many of these results do not hold. In particular, there is a difference between weak and strong regulation in the case where there are a limited number of production technologies.

PRODUCTION FUNCTIONS WITH AUXILIARY CONSTRAINTS

In the previous section we contrasted the properties of continuous versus finitely generated production functions in the context of the Averch-Johnson model. One important conclusion is that in the finitely generated, process-oriented production function there can be a significant difference in the firm's behavior under weak versus strong regulation. This difference stems from the nature of the isoquants, which, in the case of the finitely generated production function, are characterized by

- Nonsmoothness, that is, nondifferentiability
- Restricted region of inputs

An important question is the following:

Do these differences eventually disappear if the grid of alternative processes (see Figure 13) becomes more dense?

The answer is yes and no: yes in the sense that the isoquants become smoother, but no if technological (or regulatory) limitations prevent the firm from operating outside the polyhedral convex cone generated by extreme rays, for example, the convex cone generated by a_1, a_3 in Figure 12. There are real and measurable technological and regulatory limitations imposed on the industry. These limitations have not been imposed on an econometrically based model of the industry, and this is the basis for some criticism of previous models of the A-J thesis. An example of this criticism, in the context of the electric utility industry, is that in addition to meeting an energy demand (kilowatt-hours), the utility must also satisfy a peak load power constraint. Hence, if $q = F(x_1,x_2)$ represents a production function in which q is kilowatt-hours, x_1 capital, and x_2 labor (or fuel), then an auxiliary constraint relating capacity (a function of x_1) and peak load (a function of q) must be satisfied. This specification, in general, is of the form

$$h(q,x_1,x_2) \leq 0$$

The A-J model is then appropriately generalized to the following form:

$$\text{Max } qp(q) - r_1x_1 - r_2x_2$$

$$qp(q) - sx_1 - r_2x_2 \leq 0$$

$$q - F(x_1,x_2) \leq 0 \qquad\qquad (23)$$

$$h(q,x_1,x_2) \leq 0$$

$$x_1, x_2, q \geq 0$$

The constraint restricts the possible choices of input factors as illustrated in Figure 11.

The addition of one or more auxiliary constraints in (23) has a significant impact upon the nature of the solution. In particular, there is a difference between weak and strong regulation in the classical case where $F(x_1,x_2)$ is a continuously substitutable production function. This is illustrated by extending the numerical example of (14).

Define

$$F(x_1,x_2) = x_1^{1/2} x_2^{1/2}$$

subject to

$$h(q,x_1,x_2) = x_1 - x_2 = 0$$

The particular example is the following:

$$\text{Max } -q^2 + 12q - 2x_1 - x_2$$

$$-q^2 + 12q - 3x_1 - x_2 \leq 0$$

$$q \leq F(x_1,x_2)$$

$$x_1 - x_2 = 0$$

$$q, x_1, x_2 \geq 0$$

Eliminating x_2 yields

$$\text{Max } -q^2 + 12q - 3x_1$$

$$-q^2 + 12q - 4x_1 \leq 0$$

$$q \leq x_1 \qquad\qquad (24)$$

$$q, x_1 \geq 0$$

Since (24) is identical to (14), the assertion to clear. In (14), the optimal solution is

$q* = 6$ under weak regulation. This shows that Bailey's Proposition 5.2 is not necessarily true in the presence of auxiliary technological constraints. That is, the A-J solution even under weak regulation can be in the inelastic zone of the demand curve in the presence of auxiliary technological constraints.

In summary, the original A-J paper established the capital bias of firms that maximize profits subject to a rate-of-return constraint. The model proposed by Averch and Johnson has the following key properties:

- The Lagrange multiplier for the rate-of-return constraint lies between 0 and r_1/s.

- Given no other constraints, the firms will produce where the demand curve is elastic.

- As long as the marginal physical product of capital is positive and regulatory commissions do not impose additional constraints, all the capital acquired will be used.

In terms of the latter point, regulatory commissions, however, do impose added constraints, such as monitoring equipment costs. This, effectively, reverses some of the basic results: gold plating can be a rational response, and if gold plating is disallowed, say by a used and useful criterion, then the firm may operate in the inelastic region of the demand curve.

4

EMPIRICAL TESTS
OF THE
AVERCH-JOHNSON THESIS

OVERVIEW

The literature concerning the Averch-Johnson thesis is oriented overwhelmingly toward testing the theoretical insights established by formal mathematical analysis. In comparison, there exists few empirical tests that attempt to establish the validity or relevance of the theory directly.

In this section nine recent analyses of the electric utility industry are reviewed. They relate to statistical evidence concerning the impact of the A-J effect. These nine studies (all written since 1973) are as follows:

1. Emery [19]
2. Spann [51]
3. Courville [15]
4. Petersen [42]
5. Hayashi and Trapani [26]
6. Boyes [11]
7. Cowing [16]
8. Stoner and Peck [55]
9. McKay [37]

All these studies have a unifying feature. Certain parameters and relationships of the regulated firm, as derived from the Kuhn-Tucker necessary conditions of the A-J model, are estimated via statistical regression techniques.

Past data on capital, fuel, and labor expenditures are gathered to estimate important parameters, ratios, and operating patterns. Moreover, in each study a necessary assumption is the specification of a particular form of the production function. Each author presents his motivation for choosing some form of the production function, but, needless to say, there are as many different (actually more) production functions as researchers. The specification of a production function is required, in all cases, so that inferences about efficiency can be reached.

Nearly all the studies provide some evidence to support the contention of Averch and Johnson that rate-of-return regulation produces inefficiencies in the choice of factor inputs. The particular assumptions, methods, and individual results are reviewed in the following section. The final section in this chapter provides some additional qualitative viewpoints on the A-J thesis.

EMPIRICAL STUDIES

One of the earliest empirical investigations of possible bias in capital acquisition due to regulatory constraints is Emery [19]. This study is concerned with the effect of rate base valuation on the potential for conspiracy between the equipment manufacturers and the electric utilities. Emery [19] shows that only under reproduction valuation methods would a utility consider participating in a conspiracy to pay higher prices for capital equipment.

The empirical investigation is based on the estimation of a functional equation relating the cost of steam-generating equipment with explanatory variables such as efficiency, size, location, and year acquired. In particular, Emery postulates the following relationship:

$$\text{COST} = a^{b_0}(\text{CAPC})^{b_1}(\text{UNUM})^{b_2}(\text{AREA})^{b_3}$$
$$(\text{YEAR})^{b_4}(\text{CWTR})^{b_5}(\text{STRT})^{b_6}(\text{EFFC})^{b_7} \qquad (25)$$

where CAPC = capacity
      UNUM = number of units
      AREA = location
      YEAR = year acquired
      CWTR = cooling system
      STRT = construction type
      EFFC = efficiency

The strategy was to estimate (25) for the industry as a whole and then consider a partition of the industry into two categories: original cost versus reproduction cost categories. The theory would imply a significant difference in the form and results of (25) between these two categories. The results of the empirical investigation did not support the hypothesis that reproduction costing methods would lead to significantly higher acquisition costs. According to Emery [19],

> The empirical evidence, though mixed in nature, does not allow acceptance of a hypothesis that utilities subject to some form of reproduction cost valuation paid higher acquisition prices for similar plants than did utilities subject to some form of actual cost valuation.

Spann [51] considers an empirical investigation of two hypotheses in the electrical utility industry, either of which would invalidate the A-J conclusions:

- The regulatory constraint does not enter the firm's objective function.
- Regulated firms do not maximize profits.

The empirical tests were structured as follows: Assume a certain form of the production function, and integrate the assumed form of the production function, along with an assumed form of the demand curve, directly into the A-J model. In Spann's notation, the A-J model is as follows:

$$\text{Max } P(Q)Q(K, L, F) - wL - rK - qF$$
$$\text{s.t. } P(Q)Q(K, L, F) - wL - qF \leq sK \tag{26}$$

where $Q(K, L, F)$ is the production function with K, capital; L, labor; and F, fuel. The factor prices are w, r, and q, respectively. The first-order necessary conditions for an optimum to (26) are obtained by differentiating the Lagrangian with respect to K, L, F, and λ, the Lagrange multiplier. If $R(K, L, F)$ represents the revenue term in (26), then the first-order condition with respect to K yields

$$R_K - r = \frac{\lambda}{1 - \lambda}(r - s) \tag{27}$$

Let the demand curve be of the form

$$Q = aP^{-n} \tag{28}$$

so that

$$P = a^{-1/n} Q^{1/n}$$

Hence,

$$R(K, L, F) = a^{-1/n} Q^{1+1/n} \tag{29}$$

and

$$R_K = a^{-1/n}\left(1 + \frac{1}{n}\right)Q^{1/n}Q_K$$

so that

$$R_K = P\left(1 + \frac{1}{n}\right)Q_K \tag{30}$$

where Q_K is the marginal product of capital. Substituting (30) into (27) yields

$$P\left(1 + \frac{1}{n}\right)Q_K = \frac{r - \lambda s}{1 - \lambda} \tag{31}$$

The marginal product Q_K is obtained from the assumed, three-input, translog production function, which is defined as follows:

$$\begin{aligned}
\log Q = {} & \log A_0 + B_1 \log K + B_2 \log L + B_3 \log F \\
& + B_4(\log K)^2 + B_5(\log L)^2 + B_6(\log F)^2 \\
& + B_7 \log K \log F + B_8(\log K)(\log L) \\
& + B_9(\log F)(\log L)
\end{aligned}$$

It then follows that

$$\frac{\partial \log Q}{\partial \log K} = B_1 + 2B_4 \log K + B_7 \log F + B_8 \log L$$

and since

$$\frac{\partial \log Q}{\partial \log K} = \frac{1/Q}{1/K} Q_K$$

one has an expression for Q_K:

$$Q_K = \frac{Q}{K}\{B_1 + 2B_4 \log K + B_7 \log F + B_8 \log L\} \tag{32}$$

Substituting (32) into (31) yields

$$\frac{PQ}{K}\left(1 + \frac{1}{n}\right)\{B_1 + 2B_4 \log K + B_7 \log F + B_8 \log L\} = \frac{r - \lambda s}{1 - \lambda}$$

which after some rearrangement yields

$$\frac{rK}{PQ} = b_1 + b_2 \log K + b_3 \log F + b_4 \log L + \lambda\frac{sK}{PQ} \tag{33}$$

where $b_1 = (1 - \lambda)(1 + 1/n)B_1$, $b_2 = (1 - \lambda)(1 + 1/n)2B_4$, etc. The term rK/PQ represents the required payments to capital (as a fraction of revenue), while sK/PQ represents the allowed payments to capital.

According to Spann [51], the expression (33) is estimable, and this is the relation in which the A-J effect is to be tested. In particular, the question is whether the parameter λ in (33) is significantly different from zero.†

—————

†Spann further refines the estimation procedure to include another simultaneous relationship, but this extension is not considered here.

Spann's estimates for (33) (in the case in which capital refers to total assets) are

$$\frac{rK}{PQ} = .112 - .0149 \log F + .010 \log L + .00762 \log K$$

$$+ .661 \frac{sK}{PQ}$$

That is, the best estimate for λ is .661. A chi-square test showed that, at the .01 level, λ is significantly different from zero (making certain assumptions concerning the profit-maximizing nature of the firm). The conclusion in [51] is that, assuming regulated firms do maximize profits, there is a significant regulatory impact on the firm; that is, the dual variable is positive. According to Spann,

> . . . the evidence presented so far appears to be in favor of the Averch-Johnson thesis. The estimates of λ are significantly different from zero, which indicates that the regulatory constraint does enter the firm's objective function.

The empirical investigation by Courville [15] about the influence of the A-J effect in the electric utility industry is based on a measurement of the relative marginal products of capital and fuel. The motivation for this avenue in Courville's investigation is based on certain first principles in the A-J model. In Courville's notation, the A-J model is

$$\text{Max } R(q) - P_F F - r P_K K$$

$$\text{s.t. } R(q) - P_F F \le s P_K K \quad (\lambda) \tag{34}$$

$$q = G(K, F) \quad (\mu)$$

where F and K represent fuel and capital, $G(K, F)$ is the production function, $R(q)$ is the revenue, and P_F and P_K are the factor input costs. The parameter r is the cost of capital and s the allowed rate of return, $s > r$.

The first-order conditions for an optimal solution are

$$R'(q)(1 - \lambda) - \mu \le 0 \tag{35}$$

$$-P_F(1 - \lambda) + \mu G_F \le 0 \tag{36}$$

$$-r P_K + \lambda s P_K + \mu G_K \le 0 \tag{37}$$

$$\mu, \lambda, q, K, F \ge 0 \tag{38}$$

plus certain complementary slackness conditions. Let q^*, K^*, F^* represent an optimal solution. Assuming K^*, F^*, > 0, then from (36) and (37) two alternative conditions may exist:

$$\text{(a)} \quad \lambda^* = 0 \text{ implies}$$

$$\frac{rP_K}{P_F} = \frac{G_K}{G_F} \tag{39}$$

(b) $\lambda^* > 0$ implies

$$\frac{rP_K}{P_F} > \frac{G_K}{G_F} \tag{40}$$

The first condition represents the state of affairs for the ordinary profit-maximizing monopolist; that is, marginal products of capital and fuel are in the same ratio as factor input prices. The second condition is the classical A-J effect in which the marginal product of capital, in relation to fuel, is less than the input prices, that is, overcapitalization. Courville's approach is to determine whether, in the electric utility industry, (39) or (40) is the general case.

To investigate A-J along these lines, some choice of a production function is necessary. Courville uses a Cobb-Douglas production function of the form

$$q_i = m^A K_i^a F_i^B U_i^d C_i^b \tag{41}$$

where, for firm i, U_i represents the utilization and C_i the capacity. K_i and F_i are the capital and fuel inputs. Based on a sample of 110 firms during the period 1960–1966, the parameter estimates for this production function were (using deflated capital costs)

$$\log A = .7347(3.46 - t \text{ statistic})$$

$$\hat{a} = .1044(3.08)$$

$$\hat{B} = .9711(17.36)$$

$$\hat{d} = .3372(3.04)$$

$$\hat{b} = .00012(.13)$$

$$R^2 = .994$$

The marginal products of capital and labor implied by (41) are

$$\frac{\partial q_i}{\partial K_i} = m^A a K_i^{a-1} F_i^B U_i^d C_i^b$$

and

$$\frac{\partial q_i}{\partial F_i} = m^A K_i^a B F_i^{B-1} U_i^d C_i^b \tag{42}$$

which implies

$$\frac{\partial q_i / \partial K_i}{\partial q_i / \partial F_i} = \frac{a F_i}{B K_i}$$

Hence, the null hypothesis tested by Courville is

$$H_0: \quad \frac{aF_i}{BK_i} - \frac{rP_{K_i}}{P_{F_i}} = 0$$

or, equivalently,

$$H_0: \quad \frac{aF_i}{K_i} - \frac{BrP_{K_i}}{P_{F_i}} = 0$$

Courville defines the test statistic T_i as

$$T_i = \frac{(\hat{a}F_i/K_i) - (\hat{B}rP_{K_i}/P_{F_i})}{\sqrt{\sigma^2}}$$

which has a Student t distribution with σ^2 appropriately defined.

Courville computed this test statistic for 110 firms in three different time periods; 1948–1950, 1951–1955, and 1960–1966. The number of times the null hypothesis was rejected at the .05 level was 105, 99, and 74, respectively, for these time periods. According to Courville's analysis, the A-J effect is definitely present in the electric utility industry. Courville summarizes as follows:

> The aim of this study has been to quantify this [A-J] proposition with respect to the electric utility industry. The results are consistent with the hypothesis that this form of regulation induces overcapitalization. These results have been obtained by estimating a production function for electricity generation and by comparing the implied ratio of the marginal productivities of capital and fuel to the ratio of their respective prices.

The approach followed by Petersen [42] focuses upon certain static properties of the profit-maximizing firm subject to regulation. Petersen considers the A-J problem in a somewhat restricted context by assuming that output q and the revenue requirement R are fixed. The problem considered by Petersen is as follows:

$$\text{Min } P_L L + P_K L + P_F F$$

$$R - P_L L - P_F F \leq sK \quad (\lambda) \tag{43}$$

$$q \leq Q(K, F, L)$$

where K, F, and L are the capital, fuel, and labor inputs; Q is the production function; and P_L, P_K, and P_F are the respective input factor prices. If one lets $v(s)$ represent the optimal value of (43) as a function of s, then Petersen shows that

$$v'(s) = -\lambda K \tag{44}$$

where λ is the dual variable associated with the regulatory constraint. (It seems that one may have reasonable doubt about the validity of this result in that one would also expect that R, revenue, should be a function of s. Petersen neglects this point.)

The result (44) is the basis of Petersen's empirical tests. In particular, (44) shows that as s decreases, the cost of producing q units of output increases. Petersen's approach is to relate *tightness* of regulation with the cost of production. According to Petersen, if the A-J effect is viable, then one should observe relatively higher costs in those regions with tighter regulation. The three measures of tightness considered by Petersen are

1. Whether or not a state was regulated by a formal commission.
2. Whether the rate base valuation was according to original or fair value methods. (It is asserted by Petersen, based on other references, that original cost valuation provides *tighter* regulation.)
3. What the difference between the cost of capital and allowed rate of return was.

The strategy employed by Petersen was to determine a functional relationship for two different dependent variables: production cost and percent of total unit cost allocated to capital. As in similar studies, these functional relationships were empirically derived production and cost functions of the electric utility industry. Petersen considered 56 different steam-generating plants which experienced significant expansion in the period 1960–1965, and the data used corresponded to observations in the subsequent 3-year period 1966–1968.

The cost of production was not only related to inputs such as capital, labor, and fuel, but also included were a quantification of Petersen's three measures of tightness. Dummy variables, equal to 0 or 1, corresponded to whether a plant was located in a state with a formal regulatory commission and whether the rate base valuation was on an original or fair value basis.

The difference between the cost of capital and allowed return was treated as an ordinary (continuous) explanatory variable. The regression pertaining to the percent of unit cost attributed to capital was constructed in a similar fashion.

The results of the statistical regression, according to Petersen, showed, in general, that (44) was valid, or the A-J effect existed. This conclusion was reached by observing that the signs of the estimated coefficients for measures (1) and (3) were consistent with hypothesis (44); that is, increasing tightness leads to higher cost with more unit cost attributed to capital. Both measures (1) and (3) had significant t values (approximately $t = 3.00$), but measure (2) seemed to have no significant impact. Petersen summarizes as follows:

> The evidence supports the hypotheses. Using both a modified Cobb-Douglas and the more general form of the cost function, it is found that as regulation tightens, unit costs increase. The result is statistically significant using the state commission versus no state commission dichotomy and also using the continuous measure of the allowed return minus the cost of capital. It is also found that the percent of cost going to capital increases with more stringent regulation.

The empirical work of Hayashi and Trapani [26] focuses on the relationship between capital-labor ratios and the corresponding capital cost-labor cost ratio in the electric utility industry. The motivation for the analysis is the classical result in the A-J model

$$\frac{f_K}{f_L} < \frac{r}{w} \tag{45}$$

where f is the production function, K and L are capital and labor, f_K and f_L are the marginal products, and r and w are the factor prices for capital and labor. Moreover, based on earlier work by McNicol [38], Hayashi and Trapani show that under certain assumptions

$$\frac{\partial(K/L)}{\partial(w/r)} < 0 \tag{46}$$

This nonintuitive result means that an increase in the relative price of labor to capital leads to a decrease in the capital-labor ratio. The explanation of this result is seen in the structure of the A-J model:

$$\begin{aligned} \text{Max } & R(q) - rk - wL \\ & R(q) - wL \le sk \\ & q = f(K, L) \\ & q, \, K, \, L \ge 0 \end{aligned} \tag{47}$$

As one perturbs the parameter r in (47), there is no corresponding change in s, the allowed return. Hayashi and Trapani argue that, in general, s is a function of r; for example, $s = r + d$, where d is positive. Hayashi and Trapani conclude that this plausible modification casts considerable doubt on the validity and usefulness of (46).

Hayashi and Trapani show that for $s = r + d$ the sign of (46) depends on whether $wL^* \gtrless rK^*$; that is, when $rK^* > wL^*$, the sign is positive and vice versa. In the electric utility industry one surely expects the capital cost to be greater than the labor component. Hence, the counterintuitive result in the classical A-J model is modified to a more standard form.

The empirical investigation in this study centered on data in the period 1965–1969 relating the capital-labor ratios for 34 privately owned electric utilities and their corresponding factor prices along with certain measures of regulation. Two different production functions were used: Cobb-Douglas and constant elasticity of substitution. These two production functions result in regression equations of the form

$$\frac{K}{L} = \text{constant} + a_1 \frac{w}{r} + a_2 s + \text{other terms}$$

and

$$\log \frac{k}{L} = \text{constant} + b_1 \log \frac{w}{r} + b_2 \log s + \text{other terms}$$

where s is the allowed rate of return. These two models were applied to both the classical A-J formulation as well as the modification as suggested by Hayashi and Trapani. The questions posed by Hayashi and Trapani are

1. Whether or not the firm produces with a capital-labor ratio greater than the cost-minimizing one
2. Whether or not tightening regulation increases the distortion in the firm's choice of productive inputs
3. Whether or not rising costs of nonbase inputs (fuel, labor) cause the firm to produce more efficiently

For the modified form of the A-J model, the results showed that the coefficients $\hat{a}_2$ and $\hat{b}_2$ were significantly negative, while $\hat{a}_1$ and $\hat{b}_1$ were significantly positive. Hence, as s decreases, the capital-labor ratio increases, and as w/r increases, then so does the capital-labor ratio. According to Hayashi and Trapani, these comparative static properties are consistent with their modified form of the behavior of the regulated monopoly. They conclude as follows:

> The results of estimating the model are consistent with propositions [1] and [2], however, [3] cannot be confirmed in our analysis. It is shown here how this may occur if the regulators permit the allowable rate of return to increase with increases in the market cost of capital, a seemingly plausible variation of the basic Averch-Johnson model. In addition, this paper adds to the empirical evidence that regulation in the electric utility industry is effective and that the induced economic inefficiency of rate of return regulation may be a serious cost borne by the customers of the regulated utilities.

The empirical investigation by Boyes [11] shows no bias due to the A-J effect. The strategy employed by Boyes follows the recurring theme of assuming some a priori production function and statistically estimating the appropriate parameters. In the study by Boyes, the chosen production function is the constant ratio of elasticity of substitution (CRES) using four inputs: capital, labor, fuel, and maintenance.

Based on the first-order necessary condition of the classical A-J model and the specification of the production function, Boyes derives (necessary) conditions for optimality of the factor inputs. Denoting the capital, fuel, labor, and maintenance inputs as K, F, L, and M, Boyes derives four closed-form expressions denoting the derived demand for the inputs:

$$\log K = f_1(\lambda, \text{production parameters})$$

$$\log F = f_2(\text{production parameters})$$

$$\log L = f_3 \text{ (production parameters)}$$

$$\log M = f_4 \text{ (production parameters)}$$

where λ is the dual variable associated with the regulatory constraint.

The strategy employed by Boyes is simply to determine the best fit of this simultaneous set of equations based on data from 60 steam-generating plants between 1957 and 1964. The test of the A-J effect is whether the estimated λ is essentially zero or significantly greater than zero. The estimation procedure for the simultaneous system apparently consisted of a sequential search over $\lambda \in [0,1]$. One chooses a value of λ, say $\lambda = .14$, and then proceeds to use a two-stage, least-squares procedure for estimating the parameters in the four equation system. A particular choice of λ, then, leads to a particular coefficient of determination R^2 for the estimated system. That choice of λ which yields the largest R^2 value is the most likely estimate of λ.

In Boyes's words,

> So to maximize over the entire parameter space we choose alternative values of λ and obtain the result from applying two stage least squares at each value of λ. At the value of λ which minimizes the calculated error variance, the estimates of the remaining linear parameters will be maximum likelihood estimates.

The result of Boyes's estimation procedure produces a maximum likelihood estimator of $\lambda^* = .02$. Boyes states that

> Application of the model to individual plant data from the electric power industry did not produce results supportive of the Averch-Johnson thesis. . . . The likelihood ratio test does not lead to rejection of the hypothesis $\lambda = 0$ at even the .10 level.

Thomas Cowing[16] uses a different approach from the others, emphasizing profit functions. By assuming price as given, the A-J model

$$\text{Max } pf(K,L) - wL - rK$$

$$\text{s.t. } pf(K,L) - wL - sK \leq 0$$

can be converted to

$$\text{Max } \pi(K,L) = f(K,L) - w'L - r'K$$

$$\text{s.t. } f(K,L) - w'L - s'K \leq 0$$

by dividing through by p. The first-order Kuhn-Tucker conditions are

$$\lambda = \frac{r' - f_K}{s' - f_K}$$

Expanding his model to include fuel, letting f' be the fuel price divided by p and F

the adjusted fuel quantity, he showed that

$$\pi = \pi(f', w', r', s')$$

$$-F = \frac{\pi_{f'} \, \pi_{r'}}{\pi_{r'} + \pi_{s'}}$$

$$-L = \frac{\pi_{w'} \pi_{r'}}{\pi_{r'} + \pi_{s'}}$$ (48)

$$-K = \pi_{r'}$$

and

$$\lambda = \frac{-\pi_{s'}}{\pi_{r'}}$$

Using a second-order Taylor series approximation to the profit function and substituting into (48), Cowing estimates $\pi_{s'}$ and $\pi_{r'}$. This allows him to then calculate λ. The reason for going through such complex calculations to indirectly derive λ is that λ is not observable and differs from firm to firm. Spann, for example, calculates an "average" value of λ. On page 241, Cowing says "the assumption of a constant λ [across all firms] is likely to lead to a specification error and, hence, in a biased test of regulatory effectiveness."

Cowing used data on 114 plants. He removed the effects of technological change by estimating the equations for three separate epochs with technological similarity: 1947–1950, 1955–1959, and 1960–1965. The results may be summarized as follows:

Results of Tests for $\lambda > 0$	
Period	Results
1947–1950	1 of 21 firms significant
1955–1959	12 of 26 firms significant
1960–1965	17 of 23 firms significant

This would imply that regulatory constraints seem to be binding in 1960–1965 and not binding in 1947–1950.

The Stoner and Peck [55] study, entitled "The Diffusion of Technological Innovations Among Privately-Owned Electric Utilities, 1950–1975," deals with a number of issues, one of which is the Averch-Johnson thesis. The basis of the study is a survey of 117 Class A and B utilities concerning the adoption of technological innovation and possible factors which influence the rate of adoption. Some of the (capital-intensive) technological innovations include

1. Pressurized furnaces
2. Welded wall boiler

3. Nonmotor boiler feed pump drive

4. Inner gas-cooled stator

Based on the results of 66 responses from the 117 utilities, a regression equation was constructed which relates the delay D_{ij} of utility j in implementing innovation i, $i = 1, 20$ and $j = 1, 66$. The general form of the regression is as follows:

$$D_{ij} = d_0 + d_{i1}S_j + d_{i2}L_j + d_{i3}F_j + \text{other terms} \qquad (49)$$

where D_{ij} = delay in months before adopting innovation i by utility j

S_j = size of utility j

L_j = average labor cost of utility j

F_j = average fuel cost of utility j

Some of the measures of regulatory tightness used in the regression include the difference between the cost of capital and allowed rate of return RAJ and a 0–1 dummy variable RD indicating whether valuation was by original cost or fair value.

The overall idea in the Stoner and Peck study is to characterize technological innovation with certain practices of the electric utility. Which utilities, for example, are the most aggressive about implementing new technology? Does firm size or regulatory pressures affect the diffusion process? The characterization is contained in the signs and significance of the estimated parameters in (49). In particular, the coefficients of RAJ and RD would, roughly, reflect the impact of regulation on technological innovation.

According to Stoner and Peck,

In a dynamic setting, an important result of the A-J effect is to encourage the introduction of capital-intensive innovations at the expense of labor and fuel-intensive ones. The bias will be greater the more "tightly regulated" the utility. Therefore, if we include RAJ as a variable in the delay [regression] model, we would expect its sign to be positive in the case of capital-intensive innovations, and negative [or nonsignificant] in the case of capital-saving innovation. In other words, tightly regulated utilities are hypothesized to be, on average, faster adopters of capital-intensive innovations. . . . In order to corroborate the A-J effect, our test will require a positive sign on RAJ in the case of capital-intensive innovations, and a negative [or nonsignificant] sign in the case of capital-saving innovations.

The regression equation (49) was estimated separately for each of the 20 different technological innovations. The results were disappointing. The range of the R^2 values was .09 to .45. Despite the fact that the sign of RD was correct in 15 of the cases, the parameter estimate associated with RD was significant (at the .05 level) in only 2 of them. Similar results were obtained for the RAJ measure of regulation on technological innovation. The sign of RAJ was positive in 8 of the 11 capital-intensive innovations, but only 2 were significant. Futhermore, the sign of RAJ was positive in about one-half of the labor-intensive innovations.

It would appear that the results of the Stoner and Peck study tend to negate the influence of the A-J effect in the choice of new technology. Stoner and Peck's own conclusion is somewhat ambiguous: "These findings represent weak support for our dynamic interpretation of the Averch-Johnson thesis." (The ambiguity is whether weak means none or some.)

Because a plant may have a low capacity factor due to maintenance problems in the given year or because there may be overconstruction due to uncertainties in demand, McKay [37] examines a purely engineering decision in which the A-J effect could occur. His approach is to compare the heat rate versus capital input using engineering relations. He estimated the following equation:

$$\log \frac{\text{equipment cost}}{\text{unit capacity}} = A + a(\text{coal dummy})$$

$$+ b \log(\text{unit size})$$

$$+ c \log(\text{number of units in plant})$$

$$+ d \log(\text{heat rate minus asymptotic heat rate})$$

where the asymptotic heat rate is 6000 Btu/kWh or 57% efficiency. McKay found that unit costs explained none of the variation in heat rates. The variation is due mostly to economies of scale in plant size.

COMMENTS ON THE EMPIRICAL STUDIES

All the tests of the A-J hypothesis that have been described use a reduced-form representation of the production function except for McKay. The reduced-form representation is either explicit or implicit in the equations estimated. Given a standard production function using an index of fuel prices, such as dollars per 1 million Btu, without a separate representation of the fuel choice decision, a model tends to exhibit perverse behavior that can look like the A-J effect. For example, as more coal, instead of oil, is used, this fuel price index declines, while the proportion of expenditures on capital increases. The decline occurs because the less expensive fuels require more equipment for material handling and pollution control. The distinction is not just coal versus other fuels but among all fuels and coal types. Low-sulfur coal is more expensive than higher-sulfur coal and requires a smaller capital expenditure since scrubbers are not required.

Lignite is the cheapest coal but requires the largest materials handling expenditures. It is more expensive not only because of the larger volume per British thermal unit but also because it is subject to spontaneous combustion. Constructing a definitive test of the A-J effect in the fuel choice decision is, therefore, very difficult.

In fact, the test that found the largest value of λ should be a tautology. Spann's equation

$$\frac{rk}{PQ} = b_1 + b_2 \log K + b_3 \log F + b_4 \log L + \lambda \frac{sk}{PQ}$$

has k/PQ as part of both the dependent and independent variables. Setting the $b_i = 0$ and $\lambda = r/s$ solves the equation. The only reason for nonzero b_i's is variation in r/s.

Another problem with the reduced-form approach is that the independent variables may be correlated with some other factor providing the seeming capital bias. For example, McKay [37] notes that the rise in the share of capital with tighter regulations found by Peterson [42] can be explained by other factors. For example, Texas is one of the states considered to have loose regulation. At the same time, Texas has outside construction due to the climate, reducing the capital costs.

The study in which the data are subject to the least distortion due to outside factors and with the potential for the most precise data is McKay [37]. His results show no evidence of the A-J effect. However, that conclusion should not be too surprising. Regulatory commissions have access to Federal Energy Regulatory Commission data on plant costs, heat rates, etc., as well as engineering consulting firms. It is relatively easy for a regulatory commission to investigate and disallow excessive plant as opposed to system costs.

Given the more complex interactions of the regulatory process than a simple rate-of-return constraint, if the A-J effect exists, it would more likely occur when a regulatory commission has the least ability to observe the distortion. The econometrician testing for evidence of distortion therefore has a difficult task. All the empirical results, except for the misspecified model of Spann, are, as a consequence, ambiguous.

SOME QUALITATIVE OBSERVATIONS

Industry response (or rebuttal) to the implications of inefficiency and capital bias as implied by the A-J thesis has, to say the least, not been overwhelming. Some spokesman are almost outraged by the proposition. Carl A. Conrad [14] of American Telephone and Telegraph says

> I do not plan to discuss at any length the highly theoretical and impractical Averch-Johnson thesis since I have yet to hear of any industry representative who has given it serious consideration. . . . I would suggest that if Averch and Johnson had the responsibility of going to the markets and raise new capital, I am sure that, like the rest of us, they would strive to avoid this like the plague.

A. H. Aymond [4] of Consumers Power Company sounds a similar response:

> . . . I would like to take a swift whack at the Averch-Johnson proposition which demonstrates that there is just no place in the world in which we live for some of the

things that come out of a think-tank. . . . I completely reject the basic assumption of the Averch-Johnson proposition that utility firms wish to maximize profits.

Refutation of the A-J thesis is presented, by some authors, in the form of certain paradoxes unexplained by the Averch and Johnson thesis. Boyes[11], for example, questions why it is so difficult to get electric utilities to install pollution abatement equipment. Certainly, this is an acceptable method to increase the rate base, but utilities are not pursuing this technology in great numbers. Schiffel[47] poses a problem that is in direct confrontation with the A-J thesis. In [47], a review of the automatic fuel adjustment clauses is presented along with their alleged benefits and objections. One of the objections often voiced about these clauses, according to Schiffel, is

> If fuel costs are automatically passed on to consumers, electric utility capital investment choices may be skewed toward investments combining lower capital costs with higher fuel costs.

This is what some call a negative A-J effect.

In a recent paper by Ostergren [41], a retired executive of American Telephone and Telegraph, the A-J thesis is taken to task. Ostergren relates his own career and decisions involving new technology and expansion within the Bell System. Whereas academic researchers are relegated to interviews, surveys, and aggregate data, Ostergren presents anecdotes on corporate policy as he knew and implemented it.

Ostergren's main theme is that the management in the Bell System has always attempted to maintain the lowest possible cost of service at a high level of quality. Ostergren maintains that capital-intensive technology provides the underpinnings of today's comparatively low-cost communications. Furthermore, Ostergren relates several incidents in which capital expansion was deferred or canceled by Bell management in lieu of non-capital-intensive alternatives, a fact not consistent with the A-J thesis. Ostergren's summary is as follows:

> But what about Averch-Johnson advocates' claim that utilities "tend to the inefficient usage of those inputs in an economic sense?" Spann believes, with Baumol and Klevorick, that a regulated firm is too capital intensive if the marginal revenue product of capital is less than the cost of capital. This apparently leads to the belief that overcapitalization can be demonstrated by applying a mathematical analysis to the actual dollar amounts of capital, expenses, and revenues of a group of companies. In utility operation there is, of course, no such thing as an absolute measure of economic operation. Whether or not a utility is making "inefficient usage" of capital can only be determined if it has failed to follow an available alternative course which, in the long run, would be less costly to the consumer. . . . The Averch-Johnson thesis is not valid as a generalization because it does not apply to the largest utility of all, the Bell System.

Although the paper by Ostergren is only a qualitative rebuttal to the A-J thesis, it points out that the extreme difficulty of really measuring the relative efficiency of capital, labor, and other productive inputs in a multibillion dollar industry. In other words, if the A-J effect has somehow entered into the corporate structure, can one really measure it?

In 1973 Johnson [28] of the A-J thesis summarizes the progress and insights that have evolved over the decade since his paper with Harvey Averch was published in 1962. One of his more significant observations is as follows:

> To the extent that Averch-Johnson effects operate, they do subtly; the firm can engage in activities for a number of reasons that seem plausible; to separate the real from the merely plausible reasons is not easy. For example, the firm may prefer to buy rather than lease facilities on grounds that to do so permits it greater control over the reliability, availability and use of its facilities. The fact that owned, but not leased, equipment goes into the rate base may also play a role—one strong enough to encourage the firm to opt for owning rather than leasing, despite the fact that the latter might be socially more efficient.

THE EFFECTIVENESS OF REGULATION

We conclude this chapter by providing some statements by leading critics and experts in the field of electric utility regulatory methods. The papers cited represent both economic and legal perspectives on the performance of the regulatory institutions.

Perhaps the most often quoted paper on the effectiveness of regulation in the electric utility field is by Stigler and Friedland, "What Can Regulators Regulate? The Case of Electricity" [54]. The main thrust of this paper is that electric utility regulation has been largely ineffectual for two reasons:

1. Electric utilities do not possess real monopoly power.
2. Regulatory commissions cannot really control profits and level of service to any significant degree.

Part of the evidence assembled by Stigler and Friedland concerns the performance of utilities in relation to the advent of regulatory commissions in their respective states. The number of states with regulatory commissions and the year of implementation are shown below:

Before 1910	6 states
1910–1920	29 states
1920–1930	1 state
1930–1940	3 states

| 1940–1950 | 2 states |
| 1950–1960 | 2 states |

Three-quarters of the states had regulatory commissions by 1922 and 39 states by 1937.

Stigler and Friedland construct a regression equation for estimating the average cost per kilowatt-hour in 1922 based on population density, fuel price, hydroelectric proportion, state income, and regulatory status. The form of the regression is

$$\log P = a + b \log U + c \log F + dH + e \log Y + fR \qquad (50)$$

where P = average price per kilowatt-hour
U = population density
F = fuel price
H = hydro proportion
Y = state income
R = dummy variable (0 or 1) indicating whether the electric utilities in the state were regulated in 1922

The result is that the regulatory variable is not significant. Moreover, the coefficient of determination R^2 with the regulatory variable was .567 and without the regulatory term was .540. Similar results characterize the insignificance of the regulatory variable in other test years (1912, 1932, and 1937).

Another important observation presented by Stigler and Friedland concerns the ratio of residential to industrial prices. One might expect that in regulated states the average price of residential electricity, relative to industrial, would be lower if the regulatory commissions perceived their jobs as keeping voters' prices down. Such was not the case in two test years, 1917 and 1937, as the following data illustrate:

| | Ratio of Residential to Industrial Prices (Per kWh) | |
	1917	1937
Regulated	1.616 (29 states)	2.459 (32 states)
Unregulated	1.445 (16 states)	2.047 (7 states)

Stigler and Friedland also present some financial investment data illustrating that the market value of electric utility stocks are not much affected by the existence of regulatory commissions (although these data are from a period in the earlier stages of the regulation).

As previously mentioned, the two explanations of the ineffectiveness of regulation, as postulated by Stigler and Friedland, are that electric utilities are really not in a true monopoly posture and, furthermore, regulatory commissions cannot effectively control profits and level of service. Stigler and Friedland show that if the long-run elasticity of demand for electricity is -8.00, then, assuming a capital-sales ratio of 4, the monopolistic rate of return is only 3.5% higher than that of competitive levels. This is an illustrative calculation, which assumes significant long-run competition with other energy forms. Along with the formidable task of monitoring the costing schemes and level of service of the utilities, there are enough reasons for Stigler and Friedland to conclude that regulation of the electric utility industry does not make much difference.

Posner [43] voices an opinion similar to Stigler and Friedland. According to Posner,

> The case for placing legal limits on monopoly profits, whether on grounds of social justice or of economic efficiency, is not compelling. What is more, it is questionable whether regulatory agencies in fact exercise much effective control over profits of the regulated firm, and if they do, whether such control, on balance, has good effects on performance.

Posner suggests at least four areas which tend to defeat or circumvent regulatory practices:

1. The intermittent character of regulation permits profit to pierce the ceiling.
2. The cost of capital is difficult to define.
3. The level of service can be subtly changed. For example, a rate reduction may bring about a concomitant reduction in the level of service.
4. Adroit accounting.

Posner illustrates the nature of area 4 with a simple illustrative example. Suppose a firm has a rate base of $100,000, the cost of capital is 5%, depreciation is 10% of the rate base, and operating expenses are $30,000. The revenue requirement R is determined via

$$\frac{R - (30,000 + 10,000)}{100,000} = .05 \tag{51}$$

or $R = 45,000$. But if the rate base is revalued to $120,000, the cost of capital is judged to be 7.5%, and operating expenses are $33,000, then

$$\frac{R - (33,000 + 12,000)}{120,000} = .075 \tag{52}$$

implies $R = 54,000$. Substituting the allowed revenue requirement of $54,000 into (51), the actual cost equations yield a rate of return of 14%. Therefore, slight differences in estimated costs can lead to significantly different rates of return.

Another writer, Harold H. Wein [58], takes a more middle-of-the-road approach. Wein says

I do not believe that regulation is as effective as it can and should be, nor do I believe that it is on the whole as wrong or ineffective as some have attempted to show.

According to Wein, the two major arguments against the establishment of a fair rate of return are that it (1) induces uneconomic allocation of resources through excessive use of capital and (2) provides no incentive for good management of the utility.

Some of the ways in which, according to Wein, a utility might expand its rate base include installation of excess capacity, capital-intensive equipment choices, serving noncompensatory markets, and setting standards of safety which require proportionally more capital. Regarding incentives, Wein quotes an industry source (American Telegraph and Telephone) as saying

> The cost plus type of regulation runs the serious danger of stifling the profit motive and encouraging inefficiency. There is little incentive to improve the efficiency of operations if all the resulting profit is returned to the customer in the form of lower prices.

Based on these observations, Wein cites three apparent paradoxes:

- Why have so few (incentive) plans been tried in the United States if utilities and regulators alike are in favor of them?
- Why, if lack of incentives are so deleterious, are not all utilities at consistently low levels of efficiency?
- Why have utilities, as a whole, increased productivity more than manufacturing

Wein says that the answer to these paradoxes is twofold. First, utilities may like what they have (compared to incentive plans). The average rate of return on net worth for gas and electric utilities compared with leading manufacturing firms (see [58]) is as follows:

	Manufacturing	Gas-Electric Utilities
1955	14.9%	9.8%
1956	13.8	10.0
1957	12.8	9.9
1958	9.8	9.8
1959	11.6	10.2
1960	10.5	10.2
1961	9.9	10.0
1962	10.9	10.3
1963	11.6	10.6
1964	12.7	11.0

Wein points out that the regulated utilities compare rather favorably with the leading manufacturing companies. The second point raised by Wein is that in the period examined regulatory lag permitted utilities to profit from their own efficiencies. Hence, one of the sometimes criticized aspects of regulation, the inherent lag in rate adjustment, could serve as the needed stimulus for some utilities to innovate and hold down costs. Wein summarizes as follows:

> I do not believe that the overall action of fair rate of return on the capital markets has produced serious allocative inefficiency—the utility industries we are concerned with have neither been starved for capital nor have they been obviously profligate in its employment.

Alfred Kahn [31] considers various philosophies for alternative pricing strategies in a public utility and argues for marginalistic approaches. Within this context, a question is raised as to the influence of regulation on utility performance. Kahn says

> I do not feel competent to offer judgment of whether the economic performance of the public utilities—collectively or individually—has been good or bad. Certainly in some major respects the record looks very good. Between 1940 and 1965 the cost of a 3 minute daytime, station-to-station telephone call from New York to San Francisco fell 50 percent. . . . During the same period, the retail price of electricity rose 3.5 percent, that of gas 40 percent, while the consumer price index rose 125 percent.

But Kahn questions whether these facts reflect upon effective regulation or "inherent potentialities of their technologies." Some reasons suggested by Kahn for the previous record could include the profit motive, long-run decreasing costs, and competition or the threat thereof. With respect to the latter reason, Kahn says

> The rapid spread of interstate natural gas transmission lines since World War II has enormously accentuated the competition of local distribution companies with the unregulated distributors of home heating oils, residual fuel oil and coal in residential heating and industrial markets, and with electric companies in hot water heating and cooking.

Mark Massel [35] suggests that regulation, in general, has not been very successful. His point of view is as follows:

> The general satisfaction is the more remarkable in view of the basic shortcomings of the regulatory process itself. Public utility regulation in the United States is enveloped in a legalistic framework which provides few positive pressures for greater efficiency, more motivation, or substantial cost reduction. The regulatory process has been evolved through the inherited superstitions of generations of lawyers, who have usually looked upon regulation as an exercise in legal procedures.

In "The Effectiveness of Economic Regulation: A Legal View"[17], Roger Cramton presents an analogy to regulation that merits consideration. Cramton recounts a story of an old Indian sitting by the sea near a lighthouse:

> Lighthouse, him no good for fog. Lighthouse, him whistle, him blow, him ring bell, him flash light, him raise hell; but fog come in just the same.

Cramton continues as follows:

> The most basic question one can ask about economic regulation is whether it makes a difference in the behavior of the regulated industry. The lawyer is tempted to answer this inquiry by condensing the voluminous mass of decisions and regulations into an orderly analysis of regulatory policies. But, as George Stigler points out, the enumeration of an endless succession of regulatory actions provides proof, not of effective regulation, but of the desire to regulate.

On the whole, though, Cramton feels that economic regulation has its place and can accomplish certain limited objectives. Cramton summarizes by stating that

> The lighthouse can and does perform essential tasks; but it cannot be expected to keep out the fog.

5

A PROCESS MODEL APPROACH TO EXAMINING THE AVERCH-JOHNSON HYPOTHESIS

INTRODUCTION

The empirical tests looking for the A-J effect in the firm as a whole were not entirely satisfactory because of aggregation issues described in Chapter 4. In this chapter a disaggregated electric utility model is described. Using the disaggregated model will not provide an empirical test of the A-J effect. But to the extent that it is a fair representation of utility activities, by comparing an objective of cost minimization with profit maximization it can provide a measure of the distortion induced by A-J behavior. The decision examined by the model is the extent to which the fuel choice is affected by the capital costs for different types of plants.

Using a structural model in some ways leads to ambiguities as with reduced-form models. A structural model has the advantage that its size is not limited by available time series, and it can incorporate engineering data. There are, however, many disadvantages to using them. They generally lack the information contained in the statistical estimation procedures about the reliability of the coefficients. Nor are structural models routinely backcast to give aggregate statistical information about reliability of results. Also, since structural models are not first-order approximations to the production process, the quantitative model results are more heavily dependent on the details of model structure than is the case with reduced-form models. The importance of model structure is especially true when the phenomenon to be examined is too subtle to appear in a reduced-form model.

In this chapter, various approaches to modeling electric utilities are presented. As the results of an analysis of the A-J effect are dependent on the structure chosen, there is included a qualitative discussion of how the different models behave relative to the Midterm Energy Market Model (MEMM), the model chosen for making the comparison. The discussion is important because the question addressed is not whether there is a bias due to the A-J effect but how significant would this bias be if it exists, and the significance is estimated within the context of a single model.

The remainder of this chapter is devoted to the modeling context and the modeling details for this study. As the Midterm Energy Market Model electric utility submodel is rarely used outside of the MEMM model, there is a general description of MEMM followed by a detailed description of the electric utilities submodel. The stand-alone utilities model is essentially a simplification of that used in MEMM. Through the elimination of any representation of other sectors, differences in projected electric utility behavior arise. These differences are described, and the adjustments to the stand-alone model that compensate for them are presented.

This chapter is concluded with a description of the implementation of the Averch-Johnson rate-of-return constraint and the added structure needed to achieve the strong regulation version of the model.

REVIEW OF SOME DETERMINISTIC PROCESS MODELS

Process models of utilities have had a long tradition. Many were developed as corporate models to aid internal decision making. These company-specific models have been extended to the regional level to represent aggregate behavior for policy analysis purposes.

One of the first models for electric utility planning was developed by Massé and Gibrat [34] in 1957. This model uses linear programming and forms the basis of a whole class of utility planning and government policy models. Examples are the Project Independence Evaluation System electric utility submodel and its successor in MEMM and the General Electric Utilities model [24] developed for the Federal Energy Administration. These newer models are static versions of the original time dynamic model. The MEMM submodel has been extended to a dynamic framework by Jones and Soyster. See [50] for a comparison of the static and dynamic versions of the model.

Another prominent policy model was developed by Baughman et al. [7] Rather than using mathematical programming optimization techniques, the Baughman-Joskow model is a simulation using decision rules to search for the least cost solution within the parameters allowed. Unlike the static representation in the MEMM and General Electric models, there is some explicit representation of dynamic behavior.

In the Baughman-Joskow model, capacity acquisition is determined by first estimating annualized costs for equipment, fuel, and operations and maintenance. The fuel costs are determined by using a specified capacity factor for the life of the equipment. Next, using these costs, the range of capacity factors for which each plant type is optimal is determined. A forecast of demand growth and retirements is made. New capacity for each plant type is added to meet that portion of the demand on the load curve between these capacity factors as long as there is sufficient lead time to build the plant.

MODELS WITH A REPRESENTATION OF UNCERTAINTY

In the models described so far, the decision environment is one in which there is no explicit representation of uncertainty. During the 1960s the growth in electricity was almost uniform at 7% per year. Improved technologies, larger plants and their inherent returns to scale, and cheap fuel prices all contributed to a decrease in the real cost of electricity. The continuing decrease in the price of electricity provided an ever-expanding market and the reliable rule of thumb that capacity needed to double every 10 years. But in the 1970s several important changes dramatically altered the course of events. The Arab oil embargo marked the end of cheap fuel at about the same time an upsurge of environmental and safety concerns led to sharply increased costs of new plant and equipment. The result has been an upswing in electricity prices. The higher price of electricity, coupled with conservation efforts in various elements of the total market, resulted in a nongrowth year in 1974. Since 1974 the forecast of load growth has been anything but routine. Forecasts have ranged from 2 to 7% and have resulted in a continuing controversy between utilities and various intervenors at rate-making proceedings.

Deterministic models like the ones described have a tendency to choose from a more narrow range of options than occurs with the actual decisions. Because there is no certainty about demand growth rates or long-run changes in the load curve, decision makers often hedge their choices. As the costs of undercapacity tend to be greater than the costs of overcapacity, there is a tendency to overbuild, and this not captured in deterministic models.

There is current, ongoing research related to models and methods for incorporating uncertainty into the linear programming models of electric utilities. The general difficulty with imparting a stochastic context to electric utility modeling is seen in the emergence of alternative modeling procedures. Studies such as "Planning for Electrical Generation Capacity in the Pacific Northwest: A Decision Analysis of the Costs of Over-and-Under Building" by Sanghvi and Limaye [46] as well as "Costs and Benefits of Over/Under Capacity in Electric Power System Planning" by Cazalet et al. [13] are based on a probabilistic simulation using decision theory as the planning tool. One common element of both these studies is the explicit recognition of more than one load forecast plus the ability of the model to receive feedback so as to adapt and modify capacity expansion plans.

As the results show, in terms of aggregate measures of utility performance, the A-J effect is very subtle. Various consequences of the A-J hypothesis may therefore be exaggerated or downplayed dependent on the nature of the modeling approximation used. Therefore, the results of this analysis must be conditioned by the fact that the model used assumes complete flexibility in responding to prices and quantities in years other than those of interest; that is, it is a single-period model. In an environment of rising oil prices, given consistency of data, the MEMM utilities model would build more oil capacity than the Baughman-Joskow model since future prices beyond the year of interest are not incorporated in MEMM. At the same time, the Baughman-Joskow model would understate oil capacity additions because the model does not take into account the opportunity to reduce oil plant capacity factors over time. By being deterministic, both of these models would build less total capacity than the models that represent the uncertainties, given there are costs of overbuilding and the costs of underbuilding with no benefits in terms of adjusting to uncertainties. Also, a model that correctly reflects the uncertainty in fuel prices would hedge the equipment choices, while the MEMM and Baughman-Joskow models choose only the least cost options.

OVERVIEW OF THE MEMM MODEL

The Midterm Energy Market Model (MEMM) is used to forecast the state of the energy economy for selected future years and reflects the impacts of a range of potential federal policies on the prices paid for energy commodities, on the level of demands for these commodities, and on the level of imports of oil. Models are constructed for the different components of the energy system, and then these submodels or their outputs are integrated into a forecasting system. This modularization allows for changes in the various segments of MEMM without having to alter the entire system. Also, it allows the extraction of submodels to be operated separately from the system.

MEMM uses a set of supply models for each of the major raw materials: coal, oil, and natural gas. They simulate the response of the raw-material-producing industries to increases and decreases in current and expected future prices and are used to construct supply curves. Submodels of refineries and electric utilities represent the transforming of raw materials into consumable forms of energy. Estimates of the producing capabilities of emerging technologies, such as synthetic oil and gas, solar, and shale oil, are considered as well. The products consumed by the nonenergy sectors of the economy are classified into seven petroleum products: gasoline, distillate, residual, jet fuel, liquid petroleum gases, naphtha and other products from crude oil (including lubricants and waxes), and four other products—natural (or synthetic) gas, electricity, bituminous coal, and metallurgical coal.

Demand

In estimating energy demand, a two-level approach is taken. First, a historical data base and set of econometric models are used to construct a set of satellite demand models. Each model estimates, for a given sector, how the demand for each final product varies with the price of that product as well as the prices of other products. An example is the transportation fuel demand submodel which produces forecasts of vehicle miles, new car purchases, total fleet size, average new car efficiency, average fleet efficiency, and the level of gasoline and diesel fuel consumption.

Next, the demand function used in the MEMM is a log-linear approximation to this set of sector-specific demand models; that is,

$$\ln Q_j^k = a_j^k + \sum_{i=1}^{11} b_{ij}^k \ln p_i^k \qquad \text{for } j = 1, \ldots, 11 \qquad (53)$$

where Q_j^k is the quantity of product j demanded in sector k when fuels sell at the retail prices p_j^k. The sectors are household, commercial, raw materials, industrial, and transportation. When $i = j$, b_{ij}^k is referred to as the own-price elasticity for product i and is negative. If $i \neq j$, then b_{ij}^k is a cross-price elasticity and is expected to be positively signed. The simple functional form of the demand equations is chosen to ease the task of the integrating mechanism.

After the appropriate parameters within the satellite demand models are estimated from the historical data, the following inputs are used to determine the coefficients in the detailed demand model:

- The path of fuel prices by sector and region from the present until 1990
- Forecasts of population, income, and industrial activity through 1990
- Details of conservation programs
- Forecasts of solar-geothermal consumption

As the constant elasticity demand model is only an approximation to the detailed demand model, an estimate of the 1985 equilibrium prices and a straight line between these prices and current prices are used to estimate an initial set of quantities. Several other sets of linear price paths are used to derive more quantity estimates. All the price and quantity pairs are then used to estimate the elasticities used in the constant elasticity model.

Transportation

The components of the system just described, supply sources, conversion processes, and demand locations, are tied together by a transportation network that moves raw materials or products from where they are produced to where they are consumed or are used to produce other energy products.

Integration

The supply functions, the transportation networks, demand functions, and the conversion activities are integrated by MEMM to compute a *partial equilibrium* solution (ceterus paribus on the macroeconomy) of the mathematical representation of the energy economy. The goal is to find a price vector p such that the vector of demand equals the vector of supplies, $D(p) = S(p)$.

The supply of each raw material is modeled with a regional structure that captures the unique characteristics of its resource base, and there are specific regional definitions for conversion and demand activities. There are 12 oil (8, 9, and 10 are combined) and 13 (8 and 9 are combined) gas regions based on

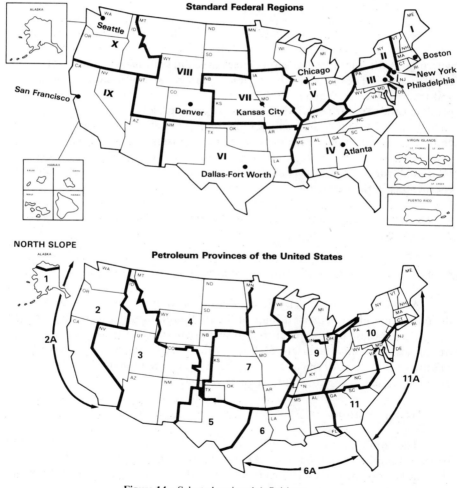

Figure 14   Selected regional definitions.

National Petroleum Council (NPC) regions and special Alaskan regions. The refinery regions are the 7 Petroleum Administration for Defense Districts, or PADDs. For ease in modeling, the utility and demand regions are the same, the 10 federal regions. Unlike regions supplying other forms of energy, a utility region may serve only its corresponding demand region. Some of the regional definitions are shown in Figure 14.

The solution procedure for finding an equilibrium involves iteratively solving a sequence of linear programs. A sequence of step-function approximations to the demand function are inserted into a linear program containing the supply curves and the models of conversion activities. The step-function approximations to the demand curves ignore the effects of the price of one product on the demands for other products; for example, only the natural gas price affects natural gas demand. At every iteration, the linear program is solved with the objective of maximizing the area under the difference between the demand and supply curves. The maximization is mathematically equivalent to finding where the supply and discretized demand curves intersect. (This equivalence would not hold if we were to use the full demand model with cross elasticities in maximizing the area.) The equilibration mechanism then measures how close the prices and quantities are to being on the complete MEMM demand function containing the cross-price effects. If the linear program quantities are not within 1% of the demand function quantities evaluated at the prices taken form the linear program, the equilibration process continues with a new demand function approximation. The approximation to the demand function described here is solely a computational device used to find the equilibrium between the MEMM supply representation and the MEMM demand model and does not influence what the final equilibrium solution is, beyond convergence tolerance.

ELECTRIC UTILITY SUBMODEL

Basic Model Structure

The objective of the electric utility submodel in MEMM is to simulate capital stock accumulation, operations, fuel consumption, and capacity allocation for a typical day during the target year. This is done within the context of the previously mentioned energy sectors.

As described in Chapter 1, the patterns of electricity use are important, as electricity cannot be inventoried. This model, like most aggregate models, makes use of certain standard techniques of utility engineers for characterizing the cyclic behavior of electricity demand. That is, the load duration curve, as described in Chapter 1, is used to represent demand fluctuations.

The load duration curve is constructed for a particular consuming region by measuring the actual demand for power (in megawatts) which occurs in each of the 8760 hr in a given year. The idea is to reorder these loads according to decreasing intensity. This information is presented in the form of a graph of decreasing magnitudes of megawatt demand, as shown in Figure 15. The point labeled P represents the peak demand, which is the maximum that occurs throughout the year, and the point labeled A represents the average demand. The area under the curve represents the consumption of energy (megawatt-hours) for the 1-year period. It is important to realize that many different load duration curves would give rise to identical total energy requirements for the year. An example of this would be a load duration curve with a constant demand of A MW throughout the year.

A good way to understand the nature of the load duration curve is to examine the consequences of load management. If point P can be decreased by a variable pricing scheme, then a more uniform level of demand will be obtained, reducing capacity requirements. The ratio of P to A is about 1.7 nationwide (although this peak to average load factor shows substantial regional variation).

The electric utility model has 10 regions that correspond directly with the 10 demand regions. For example, federal region 1 corresponds to the six New England states, while federal region 2 is comprised of New York and New Jersey. Based on historical patterns of demand, it is possible to construct load duration curves (as shown in Figure 15) for each federal region. These 10 curves represent how aggregate consumption was distributed in the past.

To estimate the future load curves, the shape of the curve is assumed to remain intact, and the curve is simply rescaled according to increases in total energy demand. That is, suppose that $f(t)$ represents the load duration curve in Figure 15. If TED represents the total energy demand for the curve, then $g(t) = f(t)/TED$ would be a unitized load duration curve; that is, the area under the curve $g(t)$ would be unity. If $\overline{TED}$ is now defined to be the projected total energy demand for a certain region say in 1985, then the load duration curve $\overline{g}(t) = g(t)\overline{TED}$ represents a rescaling of $f(t)$. A more general procedure would be to set $\overline{g}(t) = s(t)f(t)/\overline{TED}$, where the function $s(t)$ represents a modification

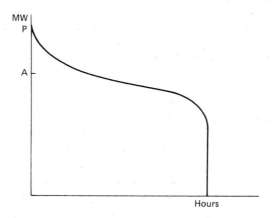

Figure 15 Load duration curve.

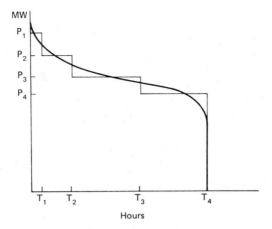

Figure 16   Linearization of load curve.

of the shape of curve between, say, 1980 and 1990. The function $s(t)$ is specified by a scenario that represents judgments about policies such as load management and peak load pricing. Work is underway to examine the characteristics of $s(t)$. However, until load curves by appliances and appliance stock data are available, any approach will be unsophisticated.

Once the load duration curve is estimated, it has to be linearized to fit into the linear program. Consider Figure 16. The function $g(t)$ is approximated by a step function with four parts. The approximation means that for hours in the interval $[0, T_1]$ the load is P_1, and for hours in the interval $[T_1, T_2]$ the load is P_2, while for hours in the interval $[T_3, T_4]$ the load is P_4. Next, consider the choices of T_1, T_2, T_3 as well as P_2, P_3, P_4 (and possibly P_1).

This problem can be viewed from a strictly mathematical-geometrical

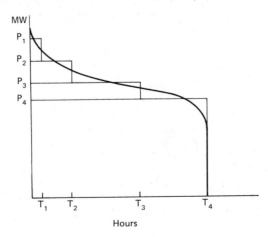

Figure 17   Supply orientation of the load curve.

viewpoint: Determine a four-step function with unity area such that the step function is "close" to $g(t)$ in a global sense. Although this concept is basically sound, there are other important considerations, which are explained next.

Supply issues also influence the way in which the load curve should be approximated. Figure 17 replicates Figure 15, but the interpretation of this figure is different; the presentation is from a supply point of view. Assume that an electric utility operates its generating equipment in four modes: base, cycling, daily peak, and seasonal peak. Base load is demand that occurs on a nearly continuous around-the-clock, 365-days-per-year basis. Cycling (or intermediate load) represents that part of the demand that may vary by season or time of day (weekday versus weekend), while daily peak load is the few hours of the day in which demand reaches its maximum values. Seasonal peak represents levels above daily peak which occur only for very short periods of the year.

The selection of four intrinsic categories of demand is somewhat arbitrary, but this classification does have considerable historical precedence. The main difference between Figures 16 and Figure 17 is the horizontal orientation of the latter. From the supply point of view, generating equipment is classified as serving base, cycling, daily peak load, or seasonal peak load. Specifically, $P_1 - P_2$ MW serves seasonal peak load, $P_2 - P_3$ MW serves the daily peak load, $P_3 - P_4$ MW serves cycling load, and P_4 MW serves base load. Such a partition approximates the real system reasonably well.

Various generating capacity types are used in different modes. Large nuclear and coal-steam units are designed to run on a continuous basis for greatest efficiency. Regularly shutting down and powering up large steam units is both costly and time-consuming since the turnaround time is several hours (or days). Conversely, some unit types such as gas turbines can be brought up to full power from a cold start in minutes. These gas turbines are much smaller than a steam unit, having much lower capital costs and higher fuel costs. The gas turbine is an example of a unit type that is suited to operate the few hours each day during seasonal peak or daily peak load. There are also units that because of age, higher heat rates, higher fuel costs, or other reasons may be cycled during seasonal and/or daily fluctuations.

In the electric utility model each facility is dispatched to service base, cycling, daily peak, and seasonal peak loads. Each unit type is characterized by a set of parameters which include capital cost, fuel type and heat rate, operating and maintenance cost, and reliability. The model determines the appropriate quantity and mix of various unit types, existing as well as new investments, to satisfy demand as expressed by the load duration curve. The mechanism for satisfying this curve is to specify a constraint for meeting (1) base load, (2) cycling load, (3) daily peak load, and (4) seasonal peak load plus certain other restrictions on reserve and total generation capacity.

In summary, a linearization of the load duration curve is used, as shown in Figure 17, such that T_1, T_2, and T_3 lie within ranges that allow the fuel choice decision to be represented properly. This permits the model to make better economic trade-offs in the capacity expansion decision.

Turvey [57] shows that (under ideal conditions) an optimal investment plan requires certain conditions to be met. If $A\{F_j\}$ represents the annualized capital cost of generation type j and O_j represents the unit operation cost, then an optimal investment plan requires that facility type j must be chosen for a load less than $\bar{t}$ hr/year when

$$A\{F_j\} + O_j\bar{t} \le A\{F_i\} + O_i\bar{t} \qquad \text{for all types } i$$

This suggests that break points T_1, T_2, T_3, T_4 should be chosen in the vicinity of economic break-even points for the various classes of generation types.

The actual strategy employed in the MEMM for choosing the break points $\{T_1, T_2, T_3,$ and $T_4\}$ is based, in part, on a recent study of capacity expansion decisions in the electric utility industry [15]. Traditionally, some types of generation equipment have been installed to serve certain kinds of loads, for example, gas turbines for the peak loads and some older steam plants for intermediate-type loads. Although break points between pairs of generation types that are themselves only loosely associated with load classes are sensitive to relative fuel prices, some reasonable ranges for the break points $\{T_1, T_2, T_3, T_4\}$ can be approximated. This means that there remains a substantial portion of subjectivity in choosing a specific set of break points from these ranges. In MEMM the choice of these break points, based on 8760 hr/year, is $T_1 = 200$, $T_2 = 700$, $T_3 = 2000$, and $T_4 = 8760$.

The problem of choosing the break points could have been mitigated by expanding the number of steps used to approximate the curve. However, this is costly in terms of expanding the size of the model. Several people have studied the problem. Table 4 presents the results from Day [18]. In this example production costs were rather insensitive to the number of load segments, because the analysis was done in 1971, before the steep rise in oil prices. When this paper [18] was published, oil, gas, and coal were very competitive on a $/Mbtu basis.

TABLE 4 Accuracy of Production Costs as a
Function of the Number of Load
Segments

Number of Segments	Relative Solution Value of Production Costs
4	1.0
6	.9953
8	.9942
10	.9924
12	.9913
14	.9907

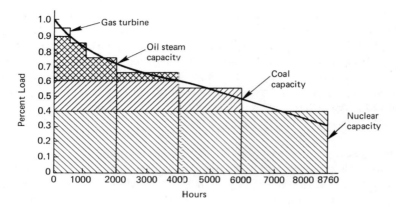

Figure 18   Annual load duration curve.

Consequently, the allocation of energy between fuel types could be significantly in error without markedly affecting the total production cost. However, in the current environment of high fuel costs the allocation of generation megawatt hours among the generation types, nuclear oil, and coal, is more sensitive to the number of load segments. A simple example can illustrate this. The example and relevant discussion are from [24], a study used to enhance an earlier version of the MEMM utility model.

What capacity type is appropriate for which step is illustrated in Figure 18 together with a six-segment approximation. The generation capacity is of four types, nuclear, coal, oil-steam, and gas turbine. The area associated with each capacity type in the load duration curve is proportional to the generation using that type.

The capacity factor of each generation type is computed for the underlying load duration curve and the six-segment approximation. In addition, several other calculations were made for different load segment approximations. Figure 19 illustrates the results. As can be seen, the quantities for base load types are stable after 3 to 4 load segments, while the peaking types may require up to 5 or 6 load segments to be within 5% accuracy. Although the initial convergence is rapid, up to 12 segments are needed to obtain a base load generation error less than 3%.

This example illustrates that reasonable accuracy can be obtained using 4 to 6 load segments with 4 on the low side. A test of the dispatching behavior of the MEMM model is contained in Appendix A.

The following summarizes the overall methodology used for modeling the load duration curve in the MEMM electric utility model:

1. For each of the 10 federal regions a historical load duration curve is constructed.

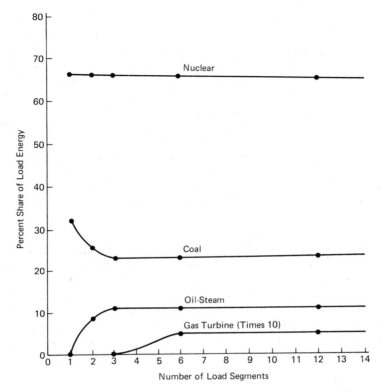

Figure 19 Accuracy of production simulation vs. load model detail.

2. Each curve is unitized so that future energy demand (megawatt-hours) parameterizes the magnitude of the curve.

3. The unitized curve is linearized into four segments, base, cycling, daily peak, and seasonal peak demands, by choosing three break points T_1, T_2, and T_3 and associated ordinates P_2, P_3, and P_4, as shown in Figure 17.

Hence, the unitized curve is completely characterized by the parameters (P_1, P_2, P_3, P_4) and (T_1, T_2, T_3, T_4).

Integration with the MEMM Model

The electric utility model in MEMM contains approximately 10 types of generation capacity. These capacity types include nuclear, coal, coal with scrubbers (coal plants are also distinguished by grade of fuel such as subbituminous and lignite), gas and oil steam, gas and oil combined cycle, hydro (separate pondage and pumped storage), as well as peaking thermal units such as gas and distillate turbines. For each of the federal regions a comprehensive inventory of capacity is classified into three categories: existing, committed, and deferrable. The latter two categories refer to capacity that is not currently completed but can be brought on line (or deferred) depending on demand and other assumptions. For the sake of clarity the modeling details of the last two categories are not presented; existing capacity is simply that quantity available by region and unit type as of January 1, 1978. Capacity is measured using net reliable megawatts of power for existing plants and nameplate capacity for new plants.

For modeling purposes, each generation type has a specified set of operational parameters such as heat rates, operating and maintenance costs, and unit availabilities. New capacity can (in most cases must) be added to satisfy increases in demand. New capacity differs from existing capacity in two ways: First, operational parameters are different, for example, more efficient heat rates or better availabilities, and, second, a capital outlay is required to obtain new equipment of a specific generation type.

No bulk transmission between regions is explicitly modeled. That is, sufficient electricity to meet demand is generated in each of the federal regions. Total capacity must be such that both the energy and power requirements implied by the region's load curve are satisfied by capacity in that region. For some regions this could cause a significant error, since generating facilities located in one region may be totally committed to satisfying demand in a neighboring region. In this case the generating capacity is included in the region where the demand occurs.

Prototype Example

The nature of the electric utility submodel can be illustrated by an example in which only a few essential elements are considered and other aspects of the model are omitted, such as details of transmission and distribution. Consider a region with a total of 100 MW of existing coal capacity and a total of 50 MW of existing oil capacity. (In this illustrative model, as well as in the MEMM model, all capacity of a given type is aggregated; that is, for federal region 2, oil capacity at Buffalo and Binghamton and all other stations is treated in the aggregate.) The unitized load duration curve for this region is given by Figure 17. Let a_1, a_2, a_3, and a_4 be defined as follows:

$$a_1 = (P_1 - P_2) T_1$$
$$a_2 = (P_2 - P_3) T_2$$
$$a_3 = (P_3 - P_4) T_3 \tag{54}$$
$$a_4 = (P_4) T_4 \qquad (T_4 = 24 \text{ hr})$$

Since the curve is unitized ($\Sigma a_i = 1$), a_1, a_2, a_3, and a_4 represent the per unit quantity of megawatt-hours (including transmission losses) that must be generated by capacity allocated to seasonal peak, daily peak, cycling, and base demand. If total daily demand is 1000 MW-hr, then $1000a_1$ MW-hr must be generated by capacity allocated to satisfy seasonal peak load.

Now let $x_i, i = 1, 2, 3, 4$, be the allocation of the existing coal capacity to the operational modes of seasonal peak, daily peak, cycling, and base, respectively. This leads to a capacity constraint of the form

$$x_1 + x_2 + x_3 + x_4 \leq 100$$

If the solution $x_1 = 0$, $x_2 = 0$, $x_3 = 20$, and $x_4 = 70$ is obtained, then 70 of the existing megawatts of coal have been allocated to base operation and 20 units to cycling. In a similar fashion the existing oil capacity is constrained by

$$y_1 + y_2 + y_3 + y_4 \leq 50$$

Let z_1, z_2, z_3, z_4 represent the allocation of new coal capacity, and let z_0 represent the quantity (in megawatts) of new coal capacity, a part of the capacity expansion decision. The constraint on new coal capacity is of the form

$$z_1 + z_2 + z_3 + z_4 - z_0 \leq 0 \tag{55}$$

Next, define the *availability* of a specific unit type as simply 1 minus the sum of the (fraction) planned and unplanned outages. (The availability factor not only depends on unit type but also on regions and various other factors.) The availability may range from 60 to 95%. The notion of availability is central to how capacity factors are determined endogenously within the model. The general concept of a capacity factor is simple: If a 1-MW plant produces 5000 MW-hr during a year (8760 hr), then the plant's capacity factor is $5000/8760 = .571$. The reasons the plant does not produce 8760 MW-h during the year are attributable to both supply and demand considerations. On the supply side the plant may be inoperable for 1000 hr, while during 2760 hr there may be inadequate demand to warrant generation from this plant. In short, the capacity factor depends on both supply and demand considerations.

Let v_c, v_o, and v_{nc} represent the availabilities of existing coal and oil and new coal in our example. Now define

$$\alpha_c^i = v_c \frac{T_i}{T_4}, \qquad i = 1, 2, 3, 4$$

as the capacity factor for existing coal units which operate in seasonal peak, daily peak, cycling, and base modes, respectively. If a unit serves seasonal peak load, then T_1/T_4 represents the portion of time that this load exists and v_c represents the average availability of the coal unit to serve this load. Hence, this product provides an approximation to the plant-type capacity factor for a particular mode of operation. Since the allocation of capacity to the various loads is not a priori fixed, the overall capacity factor of a particular generation type i is determined endogenously within the MEMM. All the capacity of a particular generation type need not be allocated to serve any of the four loads; a certain capacity may be simply kept in reserve.

With respect to the illustrative example, there are four supply-demand balance constraints:

$$24(\alpha_c^1 x_1 + \alpha_o^1 y_1 + \alpha_{nc}^1 z_1) - a_1 e = 0 \quad \text{(seasonal peak)}$$

$$24(\alpha_c^2 x_2 + \alpha_o^2 y_2 + \alpha_{nc}^2 z_2) - a_2 e = 0 \quad \text{(daily peak)}$$

$$24(\alpha_c^3 x_3 + \alpha_o^3 y_3 + \alpha_{nc}^3 z_3) - a_3 e = 0 \quad \text{(cycling)}$$

$$24(\alpha_c^4 x_4 + \alpha_o^4 y_4 + \alpha_{nc}^4 z_4) - a_4 e = 0 \quad \text{(base)}$$

$$(56)$$

where e represents the daily (24-hr) energy to be generated. This set of relationships is best viewed with the complementary relationship

$$\beta e - TED = 0 \tag{57}$$

where β is the transmission efficiency (typically around .9) and TED is the total daily electric demand (in megawatt-hours). The quantity TED is determined endogenously (via supply-demand equilibration). The variable TED initiates the allocation of existing and new capacity to satisfy four different *energy* demands. In addition to demands for energy, demand for capacity, that is, seasonal peak load, must be satisfied. With P_1 the unitized seasonal peak load (in megawatts) from Figure 17. $P_1 (TED)$ represents the actual peak load associated with the energy requirement TED. Let r be the prespecified reserve margin (r is typically set in the neighborhood of 1.2 in the model, that is, the extra capacity needed to provide a safety margin). Then

$$z_0 + 150 \geqslant r P_1 (TED) \tag{58}$$

where the left-hand side of (58) represents total capacity of the system.

The electric utility submodel also has entries in the objective function that represent charges for the appropriate costs of alternate dispatching possibilities. In general, the kinds of costs associated with the dispatching of each plant are fuel costs, new capacity costs, and operations and maintenance costs. Each decision variable (x_i, y_i, z_i for $i = 1, 4$) has an entry in the objective row to account for operations and maintenance costs for the plant type dispatched at a specific capacity factor. Other costs associated with dispatching in general are transmission and distribution costs.

For new capacity, the annualized capital recovery cost is provided. For example, the cost of new coal capacity (z_0) appears in the objective row. The value that appears in the objective row is the scaled result of total plant cost multiplied by a capital recovery factor that includes an allowance for capital and ad valorem costs such as property taxes. Fuel quantities for each plant type have entries in the fuel row so that the cost of a fuel is captured. Finally, the objective row has the annualized capital costs (appropriately scaled) for transmission and distribution capacity expansion.

With the exception of the fuel balances, these preceding relationships represent the basic structure of the MEMM electric utility submodel. The fuel balances are of the form

$$\sum_{i=1}^{4} 24(\alpha_o^i h_o^i) y_i - TO = 0 \qquad\qquad \text{(oil)}$$

$$\sum_{i=1}^{4} 24(\alpha_c^i h_c^i) x_i + \sum_{i=1}^{4} 24(\alpha_{nc}^i h_{nc}^i) z_i - TC = 0 \qquad \text{(coal)}$$

(59)

where h_o^i is the heat rate for existing oil operated in mode i and TO represents the quantity of oil delivered to the region. These relationships (neglecting objective coefficients) are summarized in Table 5, where $\overline{\alpha}_j^i = 24\alpha_j^i$. The values of the data coefficients and parameters used in this study are provided in Appendix C.

Average Cost Pricing

The structure we have discussed is a linear program. It is the nature of linear programs that prices associated with constraints are marginal costs. As a result, the price of electricity faced by the "consumers" in the model, without any adjustments, is a marginal cost in the linear program. This conflicts with actual practices of regulatory bodies where prices are set. Their rules for rate setting generally involve the determination of an "average" cost which is calculated by first summing the costs of all elements of production. This includes fixed costs such as capital charges and taxes as well as variable costs such as operating costs and fuel costs. The total cost of production is divided by the total generation to arrive at an average cost. Generally this cost is lower than the marginal cost, since the marginal cost is set by the most expensive unit of production. These average costs are used as the prices to determine demand.

The Electric Utility Submodel in a Stand-alone Context

As currently constituted, the assumption in the MEMM model is that the electric utility industry seeks to satisfy a given level of demand at the minimum cost. The fact that the price-quantity pair obtained in the equilibration procedure is based on an average cost does not alter this conclusion. If $(\overline{p}, \overline{q})$ is the MEMM equilibrium price-quantity pair, then eliminating the demand model and minimizing costs subject to meeting a fixed demand $\overline{q}$ would replicate the quantity flows in the equilibrium solution on the supply side. Otherwise, a contradiction to the optimality [equilibrium of $(\overline{p}, \overline{q})$] would be obtained.

The validity of decoupling the utilities submodel entirely from the MEMM partial equilibrium model is not so obvious. The basic question is under what circumstances, if any, will individual submodels, when separated from the other components, furnish results that are reasonably close to those obtained from the integrated system. In particular, the issue is as follows: When fuel prices are fixed at equilibrium values and with demand for electricity fixed at the equilibrium output, to what extent does cost minimization of the electric utility submodel result in capacity additions and dispatch policies that nearly replicate the overall equilibrium solution? The nature of this question is illustrated in the following generic example: Let

TABLE 5 Schematic for Illustrative Example

	x_1	x_2	x_3	x_4	y_1	y_2	y_3	y_4	z_1	z_2	z_3	z_4	z_0	e	TED	TO	TC	
Capacity	1	1	1	1														≤ 100
					1	1	1	1										≤ 50
									1	1	1	1	-1					≤ 0
Energy balance	$\bar\alpha_c^1$				$\bar\alpha_o^1$				$\dfrac{1}{\bar\alpha_{nc}^1}$					$-a_1$				$= 0$
		$\bar\alpha_c^2$				$\bar\alpha_o^2$				$\bar\alpha_{nc}^2$				$-a_2$				$= 0$
			$\bar\alpha_c^3$				$\bar\alpha_o^3$				$\bar\alpha_{nc}^3$			$-a_3$				$= 0$
				$\bar\alpha_c^4$				$\bar\alpha_o^4$				$\bar\alpha_{nc}^4$		$-a_4$				$= 0$
Transmission														β	-1			$= 0$
Peak load	x	x	x	x	x	x	x	x	x	x	x	x	1		$-rP_1$			≥ -150
Fuel	x	x	x	x	x	x	x	x	x	x	x	x				-1		$= 0$
																	-1	$= 0$

90

$$q = \text{output}$$

$$p(q) = \text{inverse demand curve}$$

$$f_i(y_i) = \text{marginal supply curve of } i\text{th fuel}$$

$$a_i = \text{efficiency of } i\text{th fuel}$$

Consider the following equilibrium problem:

$$\text{Max} \int_0^q p(z)\, dz - \int_0^{y_1} f_1(y)\, dy - \int_0^{y_2} f_2(y)\, dy$$

$$\text{s.t.} \quad q \leq a_1 y_1 + a_2 y_2 \tag{60}$$

$$q, y_1, y_2 \geq 0$$

That is, output q can be obtained from any appropriate combination of processes y_1 and y_2.

Suppose that (q^*, y_1^*, y_2^*) is an optimal solution to (60). The decomposed stand-alone version of (60) with fixed equilibrium fuel prices and output may be represented as

$$\text{Min } f_1(y_1^*)y_1 + f_2(y_2^*)y_2$$

$$a_1 y_1 + a_2 y_2 \geq q^* \tag{61}$$

$$y_1, y_2 \geq 0$$

Does it follow that (y_1^*, y_2^*) is an optimal solution to (61)?

Graphically, whether or not the stand-alone solution matches the sub-model solution within the larger model may be illustrated as follows. Using step-function supply and demand curves, either a vertical segment of the supply curve intersects a horizontal segment of the demand curve or vice versa. Ignoring the cases where the intersection is not unique, both possibilities are illustrated in Figure 20. Let the supply curve be replaced by a horizontal line. This is equivalent to using the equilibrium price of a fuel as the fuel cost in a stand-alone model. The graphs in Figure 20 become those shown in Figure 21. In (a), the equilibrium from Figure 21 is reproduced. However, in (b), instead of a single intersection, there is now a range of solutions. In practice, due to rounding off, the new solution becomes either end of the demand curve step that coincides with the horizontal supply curve.

As pointed out in Chapter 1, a comparison to study the relationship between (60) and (61) for the electric utility submodel has been performed. The 1985 Case C Scenario of the 1977 ARC [1] is the test case. The MEMM equilibrium fuel prices (unique to each region) and the equilibrium demands were exogenously specified as illustrated in (61). The stand-alone model fuel prices are fixed and independent of demand; for example, in the Southwest the cost of natural gas is fixed at $\$2.41 / 1000 \text{ ft}^3$. The stand-alone submodel was then optimized as an ordinary cost-minimizing linear program.

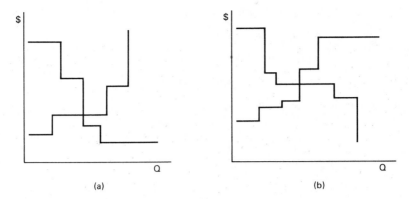

Figure 20   Alternative possibilities for the intersection of supply and demand curves.

The results of the 1985 (cost-minimized) stand-alone model do not compare favorably with the MEMM equilibrium solution. On a nationwide basis about 50% more natural gas is consumed by the electric utility sector in the stand-alone model than in the MEMM equilibrium solution. Deviations in gas are more noticable than with other fuels because the coal supply curves are relatively flat and the crude oil import price is the major determinant of oil product prices. Also, the supply curve of gas is vertical in the Southwest due to a restriction on gas use in electric utility boilers by the Texas Railroad Commission (since the time of the forecast these restrictions have been superceded by the Powerplant and Industrial Fuel Use Act).

The magnitude of this error is unacceptable, and some further refinement is obviously required. One must somehow restrict (61) to be more like (60).

For this analysis the stand-alone model was modified by simply imposing an upper bound on the supply of natural gas in each region by the gas usage from the Case C Scenario. With this modification the solution of the stand-alone model becomes a near replica of the MEMM equilibrium solution. Additional capacities, dispatch policies, and fuel use in the stand-alone model are almost identical with the MEMM solution. Table 6 shows fuel use for the two solutions

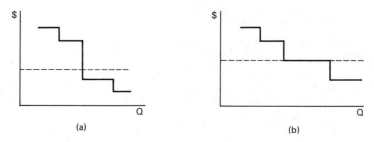

Figure 21   The intersection of demand curves with infinite supply at the prices evaluated at the equilibrium.

TABLE 6   1985 Fuel Use Comparison (Standard Physical Units)

	1	2	3	4	5	6	7	8	9	10	Total
						Regions					
High-sulfur	21	70	237	406	400	—	73	18	11	—	1236
M ton/day	(21)	(71)	(239)	(406)	(400)	(—)	(73)	(18)	(11)	(—)	(1240)
Low-sulfur	7	28	4	127	18	12	19	13	24	—	252
M ton/day	(7)	(28)	(5)	(127)	(19)	(12)	(20)	(13)	(24)	(—)	(255)
Subbituminous,	—	—	—	—	103	100	59	58	—	7	327
M ton/day	(—)	(—)	(—)	(—)	(102)	(100)	(58)	(58)	(—)	(8)	(325)
Lignite,	—	—	—	—	15	82	—	19	—	—	116
M ton/day	(—)	(—)	(—)	(—)	(15)	(82)	(—)	(19)	(—)	(—)	(116)
Gas	—	3	87	109	108	4454	135	9	206	—	5111
MMcf/day	(—)	(3)	(87)	(109)	(116)	(4454)	(150)	(9)	(784)	(—)	(5713)
Distillate,	28	43	21	213	45	52	21	6	34	1	464
M bbl/day	(28)	(50)	(22)	(183)	(45)	(52)	(21)	(6)	(34)	(2)	(444)
Residual,	167	216	59	240	92	—	—	—	311	—	1085
M bbl/day	(167)	(219)	(60)	(280)	(90)	(—)	(—)	(—)	(233)	(—)	(1038)

Note: Numbers in parentheses represent the MEMM solution.

on a disaggregated base where the numbers in parentheses are the MEMM solution. The capacity additions are also nearly alike. A nationwide comparison is shown in Table 7.

As Tables 6 and 7 show, the two solutions become nearly indistinguishable. A dominant characteristic of the electric utility submodel in the MEMM model is that for 1985 nearly 90% of the total generation capacity is either existing or committed. This characteristic, of course, is also true of the stand-alone model. Hence, the least cost solution in the stand-alone version naturally tends toward a fuel mix similar to the MEMM equilibrium solution. Otherwise, a significant additional capital cost would be required.

TABLE 7   Comparison of Forecasted 1985 Capacity
Additions (Gigawatts)

Fuel	New Capacity	
Nuclear	53.3	(53.3)
Residual	5.4	(4.5)
High-sulfur coal	9.8	(9.8)
Low-sulfur coal	32.0	(32.0)
Subbituminous	21.0	(21.0)
Lignite	8.7	(8.7)
Distillate turbine	57.6	(57.3)
Combined cycle	8.8	(7.2)
Hydro	9.8	(9.8)
Gas steam	.6	(.8)
Pumped storage	10.7	(10.7)

Note: Numbers in parentheses represent the MEMM solution.

IMPLEMENTATION OF THE AVERCH-JOHNSON STRUCTURE

In Chapter 3 the basic issues and theoretical background of the Averch-Johnson model of the regulated firm were presented. In particular, it was shown that for a process-oriented supply function with a finite number of technologies a distinct difference exists between *weak* and *strong* regulation. In this section the methodology for implementing the Averch-Johnson rate-of-return constraint into the MEMM *stand-alone* electric utility model is developed.

The remainder of this chapter is divided into two sections. The next section is devoted to the theoretical foundations (from a mathematical programming viewpoint) of the Averch-Johnson model. The main feature of interest is the translation of the apparent nonconvex program into an equivalent convex program. The following part summarizes the details (elasticities, revenues, and discretizing process) for converting the cost minimization stand-alone model into the profit-maximizing strategy of Averch-Johnson. In addition, other user-oriented details and modeling strategies are provided.

Theoretical Framework

The mathematical framework of the A-J class of models is sometimes rather unclear to noneconomists, because assumptions and notation are usually presented using neoclassical production functions, inverse demand functions, and some rarely used properties of partial derivatives of functions of other functions. For these reasons it seems appropriate to present a more abstract, but well-defined, mathematical program that subsumes the various versions of the A-J model as special cases.

Let f, g be real-valued functions defined on R^n, and let K be a subset of R^n. Define program (I) as follows:

$$\text{(I)} \quad \text{Max } f(x)$$

$$f(x) \leq g(x)$$

$$x \in K$$

Let $L(x,\lambda)$ represent the associated Lagrangian function where $L: R^n x R_+ \to R$:

$$L(x,\lambda) = -f(x) + \lambda[f(x) - g(x)]$$

where the objective function min $-f(x)$ is employed to obtain a more standard form of the Lagrangian. A saddle point $(\bar{x}, \bar{\lambda})$ is a vector satisfying

$$L(\bar{x},\lambda) \leq L(\bar{x},\bar{\lambda}) \leq L(x,\bar{\lambda}) \tag{62}$$

for all $x \in K$ and $\lambda \geq 0$. It is well known that if $(\bar{x}, \bar{\lambda})$ satisfies (62) then $\bar{x}$ is an optimal solution to (I). It is noteworthy that no convexity conditions are required for this result.

One of the classical results of the A-J model is that, under suitable assumptions, the marginal (dual) evaluator of the so-called regulatory constraint is contained in $[0,1)$. This result has a number of important economic implications. The dual variable of the single constraint in (I) (which will subsequently be defined with further properties) can, in general, be bounded, as shown in Theorem 5.1.

Theorem 5.1. Assume that there exists a sequence $\{x_k\} \in K$ such that

$$\text{(a)} \quad \lim_k g(x_k) = \infty$$

$$\text{(b)} \quad \lim_k \frac{f(x_k)}{g(x_k)} = -\infty$$

Then, if $(\bar{x}, \bar{\lambda})$ is a saddle-point solution to (I), $\bar{\lambda} \in [0,1)$.

Proof. The second inequality in (62) implies that

$$-f(\bar{x}) + \bar{\lambda}[f(\bar{x}) - g(\bar{x})] \le -f(x) + \bar{\lambda}[f(x) - g(x)] \tag{63}$$

for all $x \in K$. Since $\bar{\lambda}[f(\bar{x}) - g(\bar{x})] = 0$ [a complementary slackness property of $(\bar{x}, \bar{\lambda})$], (63) can be written as

$$-f(\bar{x}) \le -f(x) + \bar{\lambda}[f(x) - g(x)] \tag{64}$$

Rewriting (64) provides

$$-f(\bar{x}) + \bar{\lambda}g(x) \le (\bar{\lambda} - 1)f(x) \tag{65}$$

Now suppose that $\bar{\lambda} > 1$. For k large enough, $g(x_k) > 0$, so (65) can be written as

$$\frac{-f(\bar{x})}{\bar{\lambda}g(x_k)} + 1 \le \left(\frac{\bar{\lambda} - 1}{\bar{\lambda}}\right)\frac{f(x_k)}{g(x_k)} \tag{66}$$

Observe that $(\bar{\lambda} - 1)/\bar{\lambda} > 0$. This implies, by assumption (b), that the right-hand side of (66) can be made arbitrarily negative. Assumption (a) implies that the left-hand side of (66) approaches 1. This is impossible; hence, $\bar{\lambda} \le 1$. If $\bar{\lambda} = 1$, the right-hand side is zero for all k, and the left-hand side of (66) approaches 1, which is again impossible. Hence, $\bar{\lambda} < 1$, and the theorem is proved.

The necessity of the hypothesis in Theorem 5.1 is illustrated by a simple example. Suppose $f(x) = 4x - x = 3x$ where $4x$ represents revenue and x is the operating cost. Let $g(x) = 2x + 2$ be the regulatory constraint, and $K = R_+$. Program (I) is then the following one-variable linear program:

$$\text{Max } 3x$$

$$x \le 2$$

$$x \le 0$$

where $x^* = 2$ and $\lambda^* = 3$. Hence the dual variable exceeds 1. Observe that there does not exist a sequence x_k for which $\lim f(x_k)/g(x_k) = -\infty$. [The meaning of this property is that there is a production policy for which the profit $f(x)$ decreases faster than the regulatory bound $g(x)$.]

The function $f(x)$ in (I), as discussed previously, will represent the net profit of the regulated firm, and $g(x)$ will be used as the regulatory bound on net profit. The set K would represent the technological capabilities in relating inputs and outputs. As an alternative to (I), consider the following as a model of regulatory behavior:

$$\text{(II)} \quad \underset{x \in K}{\text{Max}} \ \{\min[f(x), g(x)]\}$$

It turns out that under many circumstances (I) and (II) may be considered equivalent.

Theorem 5.2. The value of program (I) is bounded above by the value of program (II).

Proof. Suppose $\bar{x}$ is feasible for (I). Then

$$\text{(a)} \quad f(\bar{x}) \leq g(\bar{x})$$

$$\text{(b)} \quad \bar{x} \in K$$

Since $f(\bar{x}) = \min[f(\bar{x}), g(\bar{x})]$, the result must follow directly since $\bar{x}$ is feasible for (II).

Assumption 1. The function $f(x)$ is concave on some open set containing K, and $g(x)$ is affine [say, $g(x) = cx + d$]. Furthermore, there exists $\bar{x} \in 0^+K$ such that $c\bar{x} > 0$. (The set 0^+K is the recession cone of K.)

Observe with Assumption 1 that program (II) becomes a convex program so that any local optimal solution to (II) is necessarily a global optimum to (II). This follows since the pointwise minimum of an arbitrary set of concave functions is again concave [45].

Theorem 5.3. Under Assumption 1, if x^* is an optimal solution to (II), then $f(x^*) \leq g(x^*)$.

Proof. Let $\epsilon > 0$ and suppose to the contrary that

$$f(x^*) - (cx^* + d) = \epsilon > 0 \tag{67}$$

Define $x_a = x^* + a\bar{x}$, $\bar{x}$ as in Assumption 1, and note that

$$cx_a > cx^* \tag{68}$$

for all $a > 0$. [Note that x_a is feasible for program (II) for all $a \geq 0$.] Since $f(x)$ is concave, it follows that $f(x)$ is continuous. Hence, there exists small enough a so that

$$|f(x_a) - f(x^*)| < \epsilon \tag{69}$$

Combining (68) and (69) implies for small enough $a > 0$ that

$$\min\{f(x_a), cx_a + d\} > \min\{f(x^*) - \epsilon, cx^* + d\} \tag{70}$$

From (67) it follows that

$$\min\{f(x^*) - \epsilon, cx^* + d\} = cx^* + d \tag{71}$$

which, in turn, implies

$$\min\{f(x^*), cx^* + d\} = cx^* + d \tag{72}$$

Combining (70), (71), and (72) provides

$$\min\{f(x_a), cx_a + d\} > \min\{f(x^*), cx^* + d\}$$

which is a contradiction to the optimality of x^* for (II). Hence, (67) cannot hold, and the theorem is proved.

Corollary 5.4.   Under Assumption 1, if x^* is an optimal solution to (II), then x^* is optimal for (I).

Proof.   By Theorem 5.3, x^* is feasible for program (I). It then follows from Theorem 5.2 that x^* is optimal for program (I).

Corollary 5.4 is very significant. Under Assumption 1, Program (I) is generally not a convex program, but program (II) is convex. One can solve program (II) by the usual convex programming algorithms and be assured that the optimal solution to (II) is also optimal for (I).

In summary, the equivalence of (I) and (II) has been shown under rather general hypotheses as given by Assumption 1. With reference to the Averch-Johnson model embodied by (6), observe that if $s = r + v$, $v > 0$, then the A-J model can be written in the form of program (I); that is,

$$\text{Max}\ R(q) - r_1 x_1 - r_2 x_2$$

$$\text{s.t.}\ R(q) - r_1 x_1 - r_2 x_2 \leq v x_1 \tag{73}$$

$$(x_1, x_2, q) \in K$$

where

$$K = \{(x_1, x_2, q) \in R_+^3 \mid q \leq F(x_1, x_2)\}$$

Identifying $f(x)$ and $g(x)$ from (I) with $R(q) - r_1 x_1 - r_2 x_2$ and $v x_1$, respectively, shows, according to Corollary 5.4, than an optimal solution to

$$\max_{(x_1, x_2, q) \in K}\ \{\min[R(q) - r_1 x_1 - r_2 x_2,\ v x_1]\}$$

is also optimal for (73). Hence, the Averch-Johnson model can be recast into the framework of a convex program.

Modeling Details and User Orientation

As previously described, the stand-alone version of the MEMM electric utility model is a linear programming model of the following form:

$$\text{Min } cx$$

$$Ax \leq b \tag{74}$$

$$x \geq 0$$

where x is a vector of decision variables that embody the equipment construction, equipment operation, fuel acquisition, and other activities of the utility. The objective is to minimize the cost of meeting some exogenously specified demand. A model such as (74) is separately specified for each of the 10 federal regions.

The conversion of the cost minimization program (74) into the profit-maximizing Averch-Johnson model is conceptually quite simple. Formally, one converts (74) to

$$\text{Max } R(q) - cx$$

$$\text{s.t. } R(q) - cx \leq vx_1$$

$$Ax \leq b \tag{75}$$

$$q - dx \leq 0$$

$$x, q \geq 0$$

where $R(q)$ is the revenue function, $q - dx \leq 0$ is the supply-demand balance relation that supercedes the fixed demand row, and x_1 is the vector component of x used to represent (in dollars) all the capital investment alternatives. (An inequality is used rather than an equality for the supply-demand balance row because the constraint will always be binding and linear programming models with inequality constraints are easier to solve.) The program (75) is then recast, according to Corollary 5.4, with the following objective function:

$$\text{Max } \{ \min[R(q) - cx, vx_1] \}$$

This is equivalent to the following:

$$\text{Max } \alpha$$

$$R(q) - cx \geq \alpha$$

$$vx_1 \geq \alpha$$

$$Ax \leq b \tag{76}$$

$$q - dx \leq 0$$

$$q, x \geq 0$$

where $v = s - r$.

The formal manipulation is complete when the nonlinear revenue function

$R(q)$ is appropriately discretized so that (76) is solved as an ordinary linear program.

Since the model is used to forecast selected future years, consideration must be given to an aspect of the Averch-Johnson model that is generally neglected in formal economic analysis. This is the existence of a stream of revenues and expenditures due to an existing rate base (most writers do not emphasize existing capital in their analysis of the Averch-Johnson effect). Revenues on the existing rate base do not affect equipment choices in a cost minimization model, but they are a part of the revenues that affect the A-J constraint. MEMM (76) is used to simulate a typical day in 1985, 1990, or 1995. As such, an estimate of the total required revenues associated with the *existing* rate base is integrated into (76). In the 1977 Energy Information Administration (EIA) *Annual Report to Congress* (1977 ARC), the revenue requirements for the existing rate base in 1985 were estimated as shown in Table 8.

The nature of the Averch-Johnson model (76) requires that this revenue requirement be entered into the model. But there is an important question of how to divide the revenue requirement into earnings that are allowed on the rate base and fixed expenditures for such items as insurance. The split substantially affects the solution to (76).

According to the 1977 statistical yearbook of the Edison Electric Institute [52], the total 1977 revenue of investor-owned utilities (all departments) was $63,884 million. Of this total, $38,724 million is accounted for in operating and maintenance expenses. The difference of $25,160 million is the revenue required to cover fixed expenses associated with the equipment and earnings, that is, the following:

- Depreciation and depletion
- Taxes
- Interest
- Other charges
- Earnings

TABLE 8   MEMM Revenue Requirements in 1985 for Existing Rate Base
(10^3 Dollar/Day)

DOE		
1	2,372	
2	6,331	
3	6,515	
4	7,479	
5	9,315	
6	4,260	
7	2,367	
8	1,323	
9	4,249	
10	1,876	
Total	46,087	(or $16,821 million/year)

The $25,160 million is what is embodied in the MEMM revenue requirement. According to Table 8, this is a total of $16,821 million. It should be remembered that this is revenue in 1985 for a rate base that *existed* in 1978. The 1977 earnings of the investor-owned sector of the electric utility industry was $7813 million. For 1977, this means that of the $25,160 million of required revenue 31% is an earnings requirement, and 69% is attributed to expenses.

These observations imply that a reasonable method for incorporating the revenue requirement generated by the existing rate base in federal region 1 into (76) becomes the following:

$$\text{Max } \alpha$$

$$\begin{aligned}
\text{s.t. } & R(q) - [cx + .69(2372)] \geq \alpha \\
& v_1 x_1 + .31(2372) \geq \alpha \\
& Ax \leq b \\
& q - dx \leq 0 \\
& x, q \geq 0
\end{aligned} \tag{77}$$

where the 2372 is from Table 8. This same procedure has been followed for all regions.

Another important element in the implementation of (75) is how the revenue function is computed. The demand functions used in the MEMM model are constant elasticity, that is,

$$q = kp^{-e} \tag{78}$$

where e is the elasticity. In this case it follows that $R(q) = qp(q)$ takes on the form

$$R(q) = k^{1/e} q^{1 - 1/e} \tag{79}$$

From (79), it follows that $R(q)$ is convex (not concave) if $e < 1$. Since all the price elasticities of electricity in the MEMM model (1977 ARC version) are less than 1, one cannot use (79) over the whole region of interest. [Although the demand function (78) may be valid in some part of the region, inelastic demand results in an unbounded revenue for q near zero.]

As an alternative to (78), a straight-line demand curve of the form

$$q = B - bp \tag{80}$$

is used to approximate (78). The particular straight line that is used is one that is tangent to (78) at the MEMM equilibrium solution (p^*, q^*). This point is chosen for the approximation because one is interested in the difference between the equilibrium cost-minimizing solution and the model incorporating A-J. The revenue function associated with (80) is the quadratic function

$$R(q) = \frac{Bq - q^2}{b} \tag{81}$$

It is the $R(q)$ in (81) that is used as the revenue function in (76). The generation and discretization of $R(q)$ for each region is based on the MEMM equilibrium quantities (Case C, 1977 ARC) and the price elasticities.

Actually, the revenue function for each region $R(q)$ is comprised of three separate revenue functions, that is,

$$R(q) = R_R(q_R) + R_C(q_C) + R_I(q_I)$$

where the subscripts R, C, and I refer to end-use sectors: residential, commercial, and industrial, respectively. Hence, there are 30 different values for price, quantity, and elasticity. The structure of the Averch-Johnson model for a particular region thus takes the following form:

$$\text{Max } \alpha$$

$$R_R(q_R) + R_C(q_C) + R_I(q_I) - (cx + YK) \geq \alpha \qquad (\mu)$$

$$v_1 x_1 + (1 - Y)K \geq \alpha \qquad (\lambda)$$

$$Ax \leq b \qquad (82)$$

$$q_R + q_C + q_I - dx \leq 0$$

$$q_R, q_C, q_I, x \geq 0$$

where K is the revenue requirement for the existing rate base and $Y = r_1/s$.

In this formulation the dual variables associated with the first and second constraints are denoted as μ and λ, respectively. The dual variable λ corresponds to the classical Lagrange multiplier of the regulatory constraint. Note that if the constraint

$$v_1 x_1 + (1 - Y)K \geq \alpha$$

is deleted from (82), then one obtains a model of the unconstrained monopoly. It is also of interest to note that ordinary linear programming duality shows that $\lambda \leq 1$; that is, $\mu + \lambda \leq 1$. The proof that the λ dual variable in (81) corresponds to the Averch-Johnson Lagrange multiplier follows from Corollary 5.4, although the proof is rather tedious and is omitted. Essentially, one needs to show that the dual solution of (82) is also a dual solution to the traditional formulation of A-J. A key point in the proof is that in (82), assuming of course that $\alpha^* > 0$, $\mu^* = (1 - \lambda^*)$.

In interpreting the results of Chapter 6, beyond the caveats associated with using process models discussed in earlier chapters, a further caution must be mentioned. With structural models, at some point aggregate data substitute for further structure, and these data are used across different versions of the same model.

Here, the same capital cost data are used for both the cost minimization and A-J version of the utility model. The goal is to determine what would be the differences in forecasts due to different assumptions about actual determinants of behavior. If the electric utilities are cost minimizers, the capital costs reflect this. If they are A-J profit maximizers, the capital costs would contain the capital bias. Therefore, the forecast with the true hypothesis is not biased. However, forecast differences are understated without a submodel optimizing the engineering design of the plants relative to the theories. The differences are understated because the theory that does not represent utility behavior has the wrong costs. As adding such a submodel, however, would result in an unwieldy model that would be an order of magnitude more difficult to build, this was not attempted. To the extent one accepts the results of McKay [37], this problem is not significant.

6

RESULTS AND ANALYSIS
OF THE AVERCH-JOHNSON
SOLUTIONS

OVERVIEW

Based on the model design described in Chapter 5, the Averch-Johnson version of the MEMM stand-alone electric utility model has been solved for a number of different cases. These cases include both the *weakly* and *strongly* regulated versions of the model, that is, two different levels of regulatory control.

The discussion in this chapter differs from that usually associated with Averch-Johnson solutions since quantitative, rather than qualitative, results are provided. Rather than concluding, for example, that tighter regulation leads to a larger output, the emphasis is on just how much additional output is provided. Rather than asserting that certain parameters such as the λ parameter increase with tighter regulation, actual values are provided. In addition, certain qualitative possiblities, such as weak regulation leading to output in the elastic zone, are demonstrated with numerical results.

All the results, of course, are in the context of the process-oriented production function of the electric utility model. A serious effort has been made to make this stand alone-model as close as possible to the version used in the 1977 ARC [1]. For example, reserve margins in each region have been fixed at precisely the levels that were determined in Case C of the 1977 ARC. Fuel prices are also fixed at the equilibrium levels of the 1977 ARC. Also, a test of the dispatching portion of the model against 1977 historical experience was done. (See Appendix A.)

The demand curves used in the stand-alone model are straight-line approximations to the constant elasticity curves of the MEMM. As such, a given quantity obtained from the straight-line approximation would always be associated with prices at or below the corresponding MEMM price.

This chapter consists of sections on (1) weakly regulated results, (2) strongly regulated results, and (3) additional insights. One important parameter in all these model runs that should be singled out is $Y = r_1/s$. The parameter Y is the ratio of the cost of capital r_1 to the allowed rate of return s. Actually, the parameters r_1 and Y are used to determine the required input s. Note that $0 \leq Y \leq 1$, and as Y becomes larger, r_1 and s become closer, leading to tighter regulation. When $Y = 0$, $s = \infty$, and the model would seem to be that of an unconstrained monopoly. From the financial aspect of regulation this is true. Nevertheless, even though $Y = 0$, the strongly regulated production function requires that all capacity serve either the demand for energy or peak load requirements. This monopoly is then one which is free from financial restrictions but is still regulated through capacity restrictions. In short, strong regulation implies that capacity is made commensurate with demand. This case becomes monopoly behavior as long as the financial constraint is nonbinding.

To summarize, there are three alternative formulations:

- What is termed the MEMM solution is Case C of the 1977 ARC, which is consistent with solving the stand-alone model having the objective of minimizing costs subject to meeting the equilibrium demands.

- The weakly regulated cases consisting of adding a revenue function and the A-J constraint to the stand-alone model. The revenue function is derived by starting with the demands and prices from the same Series C case and constructing a linear approximation to the original MEMM log-linear demand curve.

- The strongly regulated cases which differ from the weakly regulated cases in that all new and existing equipment must be used. The equipment either generates power or contributes to the prespecified reserve margin. That is, the reserve margin is no longer a lower bound on capacity; it is an equality.

WEAKLY REGULATED RESULTS

The main result of this section is a concrete illustration of Bailey's Proposition 5.2 stated in Chapter 3; that is, under weak regulation the firm always operates in the elastic portion of the demand curve. Since the MEMM elasticities are all less than unity, it follows that the optimal output associated with a straight-line approximation in the Averch-Johnson model is less than the MEMM equilibrium quantities. This is illustrated in Figure 22. The straight-line approximation is anchored to the MEMM demand curve at the MEMM equilibrium point (p^*, q^*). Bailey's theorem asserts that an optimal solution to the Averch-Johnson problem results in an output less than or equal to $\overline{q}$, the point at which the elasticity e is -1.

A summary of the MEMM demand elasticities, by sector, is given in Table 9. Since all the elasticities are substantially less (in absolute value) than unity, the

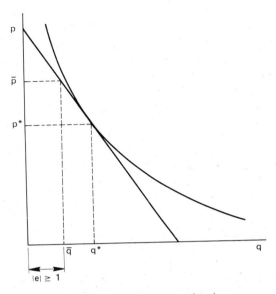

Figure 22 Straight line approximation.

question is by how much will the Averch-Johnson model restrict output. Tables 10 and 11 provide a comparison of the Averch-Johnson solution with that of the MEMM model on a regional basis. In both cases, the parameter Y is fixed at .7.

The differences illustrated in Tables 10 and 11 are large. In fact, in both cases the final output of the weakly regulated A-J model is less than 1977 consumption. The clear conclusion is that either the MEMM elasticities are too low; with the linear demand approximation, demand falls off too rapidly, or the weakly regulated version of the (process-oriented) Averch-Johnson model does not describe the behavior of regulated utilities.

TABLE 9   MEMM Elasticities (1977 ARC)

Federal Regions	Industrial	Commercial	Residential
1	−.344	−.629	−.723
2	−.349	−.572	−.533
3	−.348	−.569	−.482
4	−.324	−.536	−.470
5	−.358	−.590	−.506
6	−.406	−.543	−.503
7	−.364	−.574	−.537
8	−.437	−.575	−.557
9	−.356	−.536	−.550
10	−.416	−.593	−.698

TABLE 10   Weakly Regulated Comparison for 1985
(10^6 kWh/Day) (Case C, 1977 ARC)

Federal Region	MEMM	Weak A-J
1	239.5	137.3
2	559.8	347.5
3	764.4	453.8
4	1857.6	1069.7
5	1386.5	818.2
6	961.0	575.0
7	366.1	219.2
8	270.3	161.6
9	559.8	329.6
10	503.2	326.0
Total U.S.	7468.2	4437.9
		(59.4% of MEMM)

As these elasticities are from just one model, the question of the demand elasticity should be addressed further. The Energy Modeling Forum sponsored by the Electric Power Research Institute did a study of demand elasticities [20], presented in Figure 23. There are several points of interest. First, only one model, the Baughman-Joskow model, has a 10-year elasticity greater than 1. Second, the models with the lowest elasticities are used by electric utilities. The utilities are Consumers Power Company (CPC) and Florida Power and Light (FPL). The elasticity for the Tennessee Valley Authority (TVA) model is only slightly larger than that of the privately owned utilities. The Oak Ridge National Laboratory State-Level Electricity Demand Forecasting Model has a much lower elasticity than the Oak Ridge Residential energy demand model.

The different elasticities come from different estimation procedures. The

TABLE 11   Weakly Regulated Comparison of Consumption
for 1990 (10^6 kWh/Day) (Case C, 1977 ARC)

Federal Region	MEMM	Weak A-J
1	279.6	188.5
2	654.0	397.4
3	939.1	552.7
4	2463.5	1322.0
5	1784.8	1042.2
6	1138.6	574.8
7	440.9	244.5
8	319.7	180.8
9	646.0	370.9
10	604.2	333.6
Total U.S.	9270.4	5207.0
		(56.2% of the MEMM)

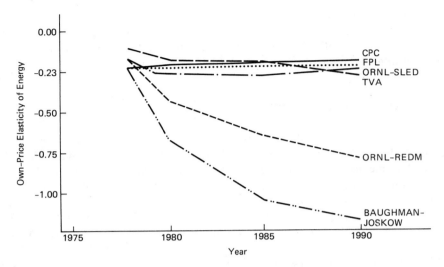

Figure 23 Electricity price elasticity of kilowatthour use from Stanford University Energy Modeling Forum, *Electric Load Forecasting Probing the Issues with Models*, Vol. I, p. 25. [20].

Baughman-Joskow model is estimated using cross-sectional data. This leads to higher estimates of demand elasticities because industry relocation is looked upon as changes in demand levels rather than regional shifts. Utility-specific models are estimated from time-series data specific to the service region of that utility. The elasticities from these models are inherently smaller than elasticities from models estimated with cross-sectional data.

The important elasticity estimates are those of the electric utilities. Whether the utilities' estimates of demand elasticities are biased downward and are too low is irrelevant. If utilities act as if these elasticities represent the world in which they operate, the Averch-Johnson thesis with weak regulation cannot hold. Otherwise, utilities would add an infinite amount of capital, expecting total revenue to increase indefinitely. Even if the long-run elasticity is greater than 1, a sequence of regular price increases can engender increasing revenues with a short-run elasticity less than 1. Therefore, the demand elasticities do not seem to be the problem causing the anomalous results. Most likely, the weakly regulated view is an inappropriate representation of utility behavior.

Other results in the comparison could include aspects of the fuel mix, generation mix, marginal costs, and prices. But since the Averch-Johnson demand levels are so small, any further analysis is of little value. It is of interest, though, to note that the concept of strong regulation described in Chapter 3 was developed only after the results of Tables 10 and 11 were first obtained. It was at this point that the nature of the process-oriented production function began to unfold.

In the next section we shall describe the results of the strongly regulated

Averch-Johnson model. These results are much more interesting; in particular, the validity of the Averch-Johnson thesis for describing the behavior of the regulated electric utility industry cannot be dismissed when regulations extend beyond financial controls.

STRONGLY REGULATED RESULTS

The strong version of regulation in the Averch-Johnson model requires that total capacity be made commensurate with both demand for energy and with peak load. This means, for example, that if the initial capacity in a region is 100 MW, then output cannot be restricted to a peak load capacity of 70 MW. All generating capacity, whether new or existing, must serve some purpose. In addition, strong regulation also requires that new capital expenditures for transmission and distribution be made commensurate with demand and that any conversions (such as retrofitting high-sulfur coal plants with scrubbers) be subsequently used in the generation mix. Otherwise, such an investment would be a subtle method of *gold plating*.

Table 12 presents output levels, as a function of the parameter $Y = r_1/s$ on a regional basis, for the 1985 strongly regulated version Averch-Johnson model. The MEMM equilibrium quantities are included for comparison.

The general result, illustrated in Table 12, is that as regulation tightens, output is nondecreasing in each and every region. For the United States as a whole, output approaches (and actually exceeds) the MEMM quantities obtained via the average cost pricing mechanism previously described.

Observe, for example, that at $Y = .7$ the total output is 98.4% of the MEMM quantity. Actually, the total production for any $Y \geq .5$ is similar to that of the MEMM. When $Y = 0$, the output exceeds the weakly regulated results in Table 10, because under strong regulation existing equipment has to be used that is not used with weak regulation.

The fact that output is monotone nondecreasing as a function of Y is proved in Appendix B. The reason is that the MEMM production function is Leontief once existing capacity is exceeded. Hence, the production function is positive homogeneous of degree 1 in the relevant neighborhood. The results of Table 12 also appear to contradict another point demonstrated in Appendix B; that is, the Averch-Johnson output should be bounded above by the output obtained from cost minimization using the MEMM average cost pricing mechanism. The explanation of this apparent contradiction is simply that the value of s used in the MEMM version is not the same as the different values used in the Averch-Johnson model. For the MEMM average cost pricing scheme, regionalized values of s are determined in a way that has only a partial relationship with capital costs because of including other nonfinancial costs. Therefore, when the A-J constraint is introduced, a nationwide approximation is used, slightly biasing the results. Even with this complicating difference, the

TABLE 12 Strongly Regulated Comparison of Total Output for 1985
(10^6 kWh/Day)

Federal Region	MEMM	Y = 0	.5	.6	.7	.8	.9	.95
1	239.5	225.5	243.3	245.2	246.8	248.0	249.1	249.5
2	559.8	467.3	542.8	553.6	562.0	568.6	574.1	576.4
3	764.4	723.4	735.7	749.4	760.4	768.6	775.4	778.4
4	1857.6	1317.7	1715.6	1759.1	1792.1	1817.8	1838.5	1847.2
5	1386.5	1352.3	1352.3	1352.4	1372.0	1388.6	1403.1	1409.0
6	961.0	938.0	957.7	976.9	993.6	1007.4	1018.6	1023.1
7	366.1	298.7	333.9	342.1	348.6	353.9	358.4	360.3
8	270.3	192.8	222.7	230.9	237.7	243.5	248.4	250.7
9	559.8	605.3	605.3	605.3	605.3	605.3	605.3	605.3
10	503.2	375.2	403.5	415.8	426.8	436.9	445.9	450.1
Total U.S.	7468.2	6496.2	7112.8	7230.7	7345.3	7438.6	7506.8	7550
		(87.0%)	(95.2%)	(96.8%)	(98.4%)	(99.6%)	(100.7%)	(101.1%)

109

TABLE 13   1985 Capacity Additions for Strongly Regulated Model (Megawatts)

	MEMM	$Y = 0$	.5	.6	.7	.8	.9	.95
Coal	73,870	30,688	60,227	64,204	73,375	79,108	83,901	86,267
Oil-steam	5,578	5,578	5,578	5,578	5,578	5,578	5,578	5,578
Turbines	66,385	30,695	53,764	57,449	60,292	62,472	64,234	64,963
Gas-steam	550	550	550	550	550	550	550	550
Nuclear	55,876	38,767	46,975	48,312	50,481	51,801	52,946	53,148
Hydro	21,060	21,060	21,060	21,060	21,060	21,060	21,060	21,060
Total	223,319	127,338	188,154	197,153	211,336	220,569	228,269	231,566

MEMM quantities still come close to a uniform bound on the Averch-Johnson output.

Table 13 shows the nature of the capacity additions (aggregated for the whole United States) for the same set of runs as given in Table 12. A number of important observations can be made from Table 13. To begin with, as regulation tightens, additional capacity (more capital) is added. This capacity increase is accounted for by coal and turbines with some small increase in nuclear (which in all runs is upper bounded at 55,876 MW). The oil-steam, gas-steam, and hydro capacities are uniform across all runs and reflect the fixed minimum of capacity additions for plants currently under construction. The turbine construction also includes combined cycle plants. It should also be pointed out that much of the capacity addition in all the runs is not discretionary. For example, about 100,000 MW of the new additions are committed, and this 100,000 MW provides a lower bound for capacity expansion. This means in the $Y = 0$ case that the discretionary capacity expansion is only about an additional 27,000 MW.

Observe that total cost capacity for Y in the .7 range is reasonably close to the MEMM solution. What is different, however, is that the strongly regulated Averch-Johnson model chooses to build many more high-sulfur coal plants. Table 14 illustrates this difference. Observe that as regulation tightens there are more (capital-intensive) coal plants with scrubbers, almost four times as many megawatts as the (lower-bound) solution of the MEMM. Furthermore, tighter regulation also results in more existing plants being retrofitted with scrubber capacity. Both of these results are consistent with the view that regulation leads to more capital- (and less fuel-) intensive technologies.

The shift of base load additions to coal plants with scrubbers is also reflected in the fuel mix. Table 15 summarizes the consumption of fuel for the

TABLE 14   1985 Coal Plants with Scrubbers (Megawatts)

	MEMM	$Y = 0$	.5	.6	.7	.8	.9	.95
New plants	10,270[a]	10,270	36,498	37,535	37,976	38,761	40,352	40,632
Retrofit	21,491	2,414	15,235	29,373	29,373	29,373	29,373	29,373

[a] Lower bound.

TABLE 15   1985 Fuel Consumption for Strongly Regulated Model (Physical Units, e.g., 10^3 Tons, Barrels/Day)

	MEMM	$Y = 0$	.5	.6	.7	.8	.9	.95
High sulfur	1240	1074	1317	1407	1410	1416	1421	1423
Low sulfur	255	190	110	24	24	24	24	24
Subbituminous	325	234	251	265	296	321	342	351
Lignite	116	79	88	112	112	112	112	114
Residual	1038	948	1178	1197	1208	1216	1224	1227
Distillate	444	513	514	520	523	525	526	526
Natural gas	5713	5232	5197	5175	5161	5154	5152	5152
Uranium	1550	1299	1406	1428	1461	1482	1500	1504

current set of runs and is in terms of physical units of the fuel, that is, coal in thousands of tons per day, oil in thousands of barrels per day, gas in million cubic feet per day, and uranium in millions of kilowatt-hours per day.

The shift to coal plants with scrubbers as regulation tightens is also evident by the much higher proportion of high-sulfur coal. In the MEMM solution high-sulfur bituminous coal represents 83% of the total bituminous supply. For $Y = .6$, high-sulfur coal is essentially 100% of the total bituminous supply. Under regulation, the use of low-sulfur coal is not an attractive alternative. This again illustrates the classical result that regulation leads to technology choices with high capital and low fuel costs.

Another difference worthy of note is that tighter regulation also leads to some absolute increase in oil consumption and an absolute decrease in the use of gas. More importantly, Table 16 illustrates that in terms of total British thermal units the net trade-off between these two fuels is relatively stable; that is, the sum of the British thermal unit input from these two fuels remains about the same. The relative use of these fuels is provided in Table 17, which shows that, as regulation tightens,

• The relative use of coal increases.

• The relative use of oil and gas combined decreases (though only slightly).

• Oil increasingly substitutes for gas (though only slightly).

These observations are, in general, consistent with the classical results; that is, tighter regulation leads to more capital-intensive technologies. But the data in

TABLE 16   1985 Total Fuel Inputs (10^9 Btu/Day)

	MEMM	$Y = 0$	.5	.6	.7	.8	.9	.95
Coal	43,560	35,483	39,735	40,680	41,445	42,143	42,728	43,020
Oil	9,112	8,488	10,400	10,554	10,641	10,703	10,759	10,778
Gas	5,896	5,399	5,363	5,341	5,326	5,319	5,317	5,286
Uranium	5,289	4,432	4,797	4,872	4,985	5,057	5,118	5,137
Total	63,857	53,802	60,295	61,447	62,397	63,222	63,922	64,221

TABLE 17   1985 Percentage of Fuel Inputs

	MEMM	$Y = 0$	.5	.6	.7	.8	.9	.95
Coal	.682	.659	.659	.662	.664	.667	.668	.670
Oil	.143	.158	.172	.172	.171	.169	.168	.168
Gas	.092	.101	.089	.087	.085	.084	.083	.082
Uranium	.082	.082	.080	.080	.080	.080	.080	.080
Total	1.000	1.000	1.000	1.000	1.000	1.000	1.000	1.000

Table 17 can also be considered inconsistent with the classical point of view of the consequences of the Averch-Johnson model. For example, why is it that the combined oil and gas percentages for all regulated runs exceeds that of the MEMM model? In addition, why is it that the relative use of coal in all regulated runs is less than the MEMM model even though, according to Table 17, for $Y \geq .8$ the regulated runs are building more new coal plants than the MEMM model? These observations are in large part explained by significant regional differences in supply and demand.

Under strong regulation, any new capacity additions must be used either to generate electricity or contribute to a (fixed) reserve margin. As such, strong regulation formally restricts any gold plating. But a more subtle form of gold plating can still take place. For the $Y = .8$ case there is almost 6000 MW of coal (subbituminous and lignite) capacity added in regions 8 and 10 to satisfy the reserve margin requirement. Instead of the less expensive turbines, the more capital-intensive coal plants are built to satisfy the reserve margin constraint. Taking this into account shows that the $Y = .8$ case and the MEMM model have about the same quantity of coal capacity for *operation*. The total quantity of new coal capacity that is added solely for reserve margin use is given in Table 18.

Significantly, the new coal capacity shown in Table 18 is not uniformly distributed among all regions. At the extreme of $Y = .95$, only three regions, federal regions 7, 8, and 10, add new coal capacity solely for reserve margin. What distinguishes these regions is that there are no oil-fired units operating in base, intermediate, or immediate-peak load ranges. If such were the case, one would question why the A-J solution would include idle coal plants at the expense of operating the higher-fuel-cost oil plants. That public utility commissions would allow coal plants to meet the reserve margin requirements is unrealistic. This means that actual regulation is probably even tighter than it is defined to be in the model.

One fact about the nature of the strongly regulated model runs (which is described further in the next section) is that the optimal solution may occur at a

TABLE 18   1985 New Coal Additions for Reserve Margin (Megawatts)

	$Y = 0$	.5	.6	.7	.8	.9	.95
U.S. (total)	0	2502	3565	4478	5547	6501	6948

point where the marginal revenue is actually negative. This happens because existing (and committed) capacity requires a commensurate peak load, which, in turn, is a determinant of total load and corresponding kilowatt-hour output. The fact is that existing and committed capacity is enough to require a total kilowatt-hour output (based on the assumed MEMM elasticities) that falls in the inelastic region, that is, where marginal revenue is negative.

Consequently, if there is no rate-of-return restriction, such as in the $Y = 0$ case, no new capacity would be added. For $Y = 0$ this is essentially what happens. The only new capacity additions are new turbines to satisfy the reserve margin constraint. The 30,668 MW of new coal capacity (Table 13) is entirely committed through current construction plans. In the $Y = 0$ case, the model restricts output as much as possible.

The preceding discussion also explains why the *relative* use of oil and gas is larger for $Y = 0$ than for the MEMM solution. The reason is that the relative amount of oil and gas capacity is larger in the $Y = 0$ case than in MEMM. Both models begin with about 540,000 total MW of which 102,000 are oil-fired residual plants. As a result, the total amount of oil-fired residual plants for both models is about 107,600 MW by 1985. Hence, residual capacity for MEMM is $107,600/(540,000 + 223,300) = 14.1\%$, and the residual capacity for the $Y = 0$ case is $107,600/(540,000 + 127,300) = 16.1\%$. At $Y = 0$, the relative quantity of oil-fired residual plants is larger than in MEMM.

As Y increases and regulation tightens, more capital is invested, keeping the rate-of-return constraint binding. This results in additional coal capacity, which, in turn, is reflected in ever-increasing use of coal and a decrease in the relative use of oil and gas. At $Y = 0$, the relative use of oil and gas is about 26% of the total British thermal unit input. As Y increases to .95, this relative use of these two fuels decreases to 25%. In terms of these relative decreases, the standard expectation that tighter regulation results in technologies with lower-priced fuels is illustrated. Correspondingly, Table 16 shows on a relative basis the monotone increasing use of coal as a function of tighter regulation.

The question remains of how to explain that on a national basis regulation leads to a greater absolute consumption of oil. The answer is largely explained by regional differences in supply and demand. Regions 1, 2, and 9 are the regions heavily dependent on existing residual-fired plants. In fact, these three regions account for nearly 60% of the existing residual-fired plants. Observe in Table 13 that total sales in the United States at $Y = .8$ are slightly less than the MEMM but that in regions 1, 2, and 9 sales are actually higher than the MEMM (by an average of 5%) due to the nature of the model approximations. Hence, those regions heavily dependent on residual-fired generation are also the ones subject to a greater demand. The net result is that the residual-fired plants are run "harder" in the A-J solution. The A-J solution shows for regions 1, 2, and 9 that 18,400 MW of residual plants are operated in base, while only 9600 MW of residual plants are operated in base in the MEMM solution. Furthermore, in MEMM a total of 15,200 MW of residual plants is retired (from regions 1,2,

TABLE 19   Deployment of Total Coal Capacity for Regions 3, 4, 5, 7, and 8—Both Existing and New Capacity (Megawatts)

		MEMM	$Y = .8$
Base		184,666	169,417
Intermediate		48,083	54,917
Intermediate-peak		1,200	5,625
	Total	233,949	229,959

and 9), while the A-J solution show only 9900 MW of retired residual plants in these regions. The lower retirement rate is due to reserve margin constraints, as a retirement is really a reflection of underutilization and not actual plant closings. The extent to which public utility commissions require this equipment to operate while restricting the reserve margins determines the degree to which the increase in oil consumption is valid. The increase due to higher demand is an artifact of the model approximations.

The explanation as to why the absolute consumption of coal in the regulated case is smaller than MEMM is similarly motivated. Regions 3, 4, 5, 7, and 8 are regions that comprise the bulk of the existing coal capacity. Together, these regions, for the $Y = .8$ case of Table 13, show an overall decrease of about 2% in energy sales as compared to MEMM. Region 8 shows the largest reduction, and in this region some 2250 MW of existing coal capacity is retired. (There are no retirements of coal in MEMM.) Although no retirements of existing coal capacity occur in the other four regions, there is a significant shift of all coal capacity (both existing and new) in the A-J solution to higher load categories, as shown in Table 19. Observe for $Y = .8$ that about 15,000 MW has been moved from base into higher load categories. The net result is a smaller consumption of coal for the $Y = .8$ case.

In summary, the results of the strong regulation cases both corroborate the classical expectations and provide an unexpected conclusion. The corroboration is embodied in Tables 12, 13, 14, and 17, which show that as regulation tightens, output is increased, capacity is increased, and more capital-intensive technologies are chosen as illustrated by the increasing (relative) use of coal. The rather unexpected phenomenon is in the absolute use of fuels as given by Table 17. This table shows for values of Y in the realistic range of .7 to .8 that strong regulation actually leads to a larger use of oil and decreased dependence on coal. In particular, at $Y = .7$ the use of coal is 95% of the analogous MEMM usage, while oil is 117% of the MEMM consumption. The explanation of this result is in terms of significant regional differences; that is, in the A-J solution there is a higher demand in regions that are predominantly oil fired due to the modeling approximations and lower demand in the coal-fired regions.

Three general conclusions may be drawn about the A-J model results:

• There is a larger share of oil use because demand is lower and the proportion of oil capacity is greater in existing stock than in capacity additions.

- High-sulfur coal is preferred because scrubbers represent nonproductive capital stock, reducing demand in the inelastic portion of the demand curve.
- Demands, and therefore prices, are not significantly different, reducing the importance of equity issues associated with A-J.

Before concluding this section, it is useful to compare the 1990 impacts on demand to see if the small differences in demands in 1985 are due to such a large component of existing capacity relative to production. See Table 20. With higher demands and 5 more years of retirements, existing capacity is not as dominant. However, in this case the strong A-J demand is 94% of the demand under cost minimization, replicating 1985 results.

TABLE 20   Stongly Regulated Comparison of Consumption for 1990
(10^6 kWh/Day, $Y = .7$) (Case C, 1977 ARC)

Federal Region	MEMM	Strong A-J
1	279.6	274.3
2	654.0	645.5
3	939.1	924.9
4	2463.5	2266.2
5	1784.8	1734.7
6	1138.6	1077.8
7	440.9	412.6
8	319.7	278.1
9	646.0	606.9
10	604.2	533.4
Total U.S.	9270.4	8743.3

ADDITIONAL INSIGHTS

One of the fundamental properties of an optimal solution for the weakly regulated Averch-Johnson model is that $\lambda^* \leq r_1/s$. This is Bailey's Proposition 5.1 (presented in Chapter 3). However, it was further demonstrated that this property may not necessarily hold in the strongly regulated version of the Averch-Johnson model. This particular observation is extremely important for assessing the nature and characteristics of an optimal solution to the strongly regulated model. Theorem 6.1 shows that under strong regulation Bailey's result may be exactly reversed. Recall that (6) is the case of strong regulation since the production function is of the form $q = F(x_1, x_2)$.

Theorem 6.1   Suppose that an optimal solution (q^*, x_1^*, x_2^*) for (6) is such that $R'(q^*) < 0$, where $R(q) = qp(q)$ is the revenue function. Then $\lambda^* \geq r_1/s$.

Proof.   Since $R'(q^*) < 0$, the constraint $q = F(x_1, x_2)$ may be rewritten as

$q \geq F(x_1,x_2)$, and the same solution must be obtained. (Otherwise, the marginal revenue must be positive). Hence, (6) can be cast in the following form:

$$\text{Max } R(q) - r_1x_1 - r_2x_2$$

$$\text{s.t. } R(q) - sx_1 - r_2x_2 \leq 0 \qquad (\lambda)$$

$$-q + F(x_1,x_2) \leq 0 \qquad (\mu) \tag{83}$$

$$q, x_1, x_2 \geq 0$$

The Kuhn-Tucker necessary conditions, assuming x_1^* positive, provide

$$-r_1 = -s\lambda^* + \mu^* \frac{\partial F(x_1^*,x_2^*)}{\partial x_1} \tag{84}$$

where $(\lambda^*,\mu^*) \geq 0$. Since $\partial F/\partial x_1 \geq 0$, it follows that

$$-r_1 \geq -s\lambda^*$$

so then

$$\lambda^* \geq \frac{r_1}{s}$$

and this completes the proof.

To show how Theorem 6.1 and Bailey's Proposition 5.1 relate, consider a simple example. Let the demand function be

$$q = kp^{-e}$$

and let the production function require one input x and have the form

$$q = x$$

Then a straightforward application of the Kuhn-Tucker conditions for (83) results in

$$\lambda^* = \frac{(1 - 1/e)k^{1/e}q^{-1/e} - r}{(1 - 1/e)k^{1/e}q^{-1/e} - s}$$

For $e = 1$, $\lambda^* = r/s$. As the demand elasticity e increases above 1, λ^* decreases below r/s, and as e decreases below 1, λ^* increases above r/s.

An illustration of Theorem 6.1 is given in Table 21, which provides the value of λ^* for each of the 10 regions as a function of the parameter $Y = r_1/s$. The blanks for region 5 at $Y = .5$ and for all values of Y in region 9 mean that $\lambda^* = 0$. This is not a contradiction to the theorem because in these cases the marginal revenue is positive and the traditional result that $\lambda^* \leq r_1/s$ is in effect.

TABLE 21   λ * Values for Strong Regulation

	Y = .5	.6	.7	.8	.9	.95
1	.8195	.8770	.9173	.9504	.9773	.9891
2	.8187	.8728	.9182	.9508	.9781	.9895
3	.6703	.7648	.8959	.9380	.9725	.9873
4	.8507	.8958	.9340	.9607	.9829	.9918
5	—	.7779	.8523	.9082	.9577	.9850
6	.6400	.8039	.8677	.9241	.9655	.9834
7	.7312	.8094	.8762	.9261	.9664	.9847
8	.6498	.7529	.8337	.8969	.9537	.9775
9	—	—	—	—	—	—
10	.5846	.6830	.7793	.8626	.9352	.9688

7

CONCLUSIONS

In Chapter 6, results of both weak and strong regulation in the context of the Midterm Energy Market Model (MEMM) electric utility model have been examined. For the case of weak regulation the model results show, as expected, that output is restricted to the region where marginal revenue is positive. Since the MEMM price elasticities for electricity are significantly less than 1, a production level of about 60% of the MEMM forecast is obtained. In fact, under weak regulation the 1985 output levels are less than the actual 1977 levels. Clearly, either the weakly regulated model is not an appropriate description of utility behavior, or else the MEMM price elasticities for the demand of electricity are not realistic. Given the elasticities used by industry, the more likely conclusion is that the weak A-J thesis is unrealistic.

The strongly regulated model, where PUCs impose a need for power criterion, provides results that both corroborate and extend the classical A-J theory. Nevertheless, in many respects the results of the strongly regulated model are very similar to those of MEMM. In particular, output levels under strong regulation are very close to those forecasted by MEMM. Because the demand growth rates remain reasonable, the hypothesis that utility behavior is described by the strongly regulated Averch-Johnson model is a candidate theory for how utilities behave.

In terms of historical concerns about the Averch-Johnson theory, the question of whether utility customers are overcharged becomes moot since the demand levels and attendant delivered prices are not substantially different from cost minimization.

The strongly regulated results show that as regulation tightens, more capital-intensive technologies are chosen. More coal plants with scrubbers are built, and more retrofitting of existing coal plants occurs as regulation tightens. The relative percentage of coal as a fuel increases, while oil and gas percentages fall. These results are consistent with the classical expectations about regulation.

On the other hand, it is somewhat surprising that under strong regulation the absolute amount of coal consumed by utilities is less than the MEMM model, and, correspondingly, the absolute use of oil is actually higher under strong regulation than in the MEMM. This is largely explained by regional differences. Regions 1, 2, and 9 are largely oil fired, and these are the regions in the A-J solutions that show an increase in total sales as compared to MEMM due to the nature of the model approximations. Conversely, regions 3, 4, 5, 7, and 8 are largely coal fired, and these regions show a decrease in sales as compared to the MEMM.

The net result is that the oil fired units in regions 1, 2, and 9 are run more intensely, while the coal fired units in regions 3, 4, 5, 7, and 8 are run less intensely. The result is the consumption of more oil relative to coal, a conclusion valid beyond the error induced by model approximation.

The fact that strong regulation can result in output levels in which the marginal revenue is negative has a number of significant consequences. One of these is that the Averch-Johnson variable λ^* is bounded below (not above) by r_1/s. Hence, as regulation tightens, the variable λ^* approaches 1. Having a lower bound, instead of an upper bound, of r_1/s requires that any statistical test such as those described in Chapter 4 have a value of λ significantly different from zero, rather than just positive.

An important aspect of the preceding analysis is that it was done with a specific policy set—no Powerplant and Industrial Fuel Use Act (PIFUA) and no best available control technology (BACT) on air emissions. As both sets of regulations reduce the freedom of choice by utilities, the differences between forecasts with and without A-J would be reduced even further. Interestingly, these regulations induce electric utilities to be more capital intensive, bringing the cost minimization solution closer to the A-J solution. Also, an analysis of BACT assuming the A-J hypothesis would lead to a conclusion that BACT would have little effect on utility behavior.

APPENDIX A

ASSESSMENT OF DISPATCHING BEHAVIOR IN THE ELECTRIC UTILITY SUBMODEL FOR 1977

OVERVIEW

Our goal in this appendix is to test the ability of the MEMM electric utility submodel to replicate actual dispatching experience. The idea is to structure the model coefficients on capacities, fuel costs, and demand to match some past period and observe to what extent the results of the electric utility model are similar to the actual historical performance. The logical assumption is that the closer the model results coincide with actual historical performance, the more credibility there is to be associated with forecasts of future behavior. On the other hand, such an exercise may suggest that certain data, parameters, or model assumptions are simply not consistent with past or current performance of the electric utility industry.

The MEMM electric utility submodel may be characterized as a model that simultaneously

1. Chooses a mix of generation equipment for necessary capital expansion and
2. Dispatches both existing and new equipment to meet demand in a least cost manner.

Typically, these actions are simulated for some target day in 1985, 1990, or 1995. For this particular historical assessment, the decisions associated with item 2 are investigated. That is, the electric utility submodel is run for the target year 1977 with existing capacities chosen as identical to those of 1977. Hence, capacity expansion is not required. The question is whether the model dispatches existing capacity in a manner that reproduces what actually took place in 1977.

METHODOLOGICAL APPROACH

As with the main body of the study, the electric utility portion of the MEMM model is separated from the other components and structured in a so-called *stand-alone* context. The electric utility model is connected to the rest of the MEMM model through utility fuel prices and quantities and electricity demands.

In the overall MEMM design, fuel prices and flows and end-use demands are determined endogenously. For the historical validation the utilities model is separated from the rest of the MEMM model by specifying fuel prices and electricity demands. These two important classes of parameters are fixed at their (regional) 1977 values. With these parameters fixed, the comparison is simply between the least cost solution of the stand-alone model and actual 1977 statistics as compiled by the Edison Electric Institute (EEI) [52].

Before describing the results of the 1977 comparison, some additional comment concerning the fairness of such a comparison may be in order. In particular, what type of error is introduced by assuming that regional fuel prices are not dependent on quantity? Fixed fuel prices mean that the associated supply curves are horizontal and, in addition, do not take into account that some fuels such as distillate and residual oil are joint products. Conceivably, significant deviations between the results of the stand-alone model and actual 1977 statistics may be due to the assumption of fixed fuel prices, rather than some inherent shortcoming in the model itself.

A partial answer to this question of the role of fixed fuel prices is given in Chapter 5 by comparing the equilibrium solution with the stand-alone model for 1985. Unfortunately, these two 1985 results do not correspond very well. The significant difference is that the stand-alone model chooses to use over 50% more natural gas than the MEMM solution. The use of other fossil fuels is correspondingly lowered. These differences can only be attributed to the flat fuel supply curves.

The experiments with the 1985 stand-alone model strongly suggest that the availability of natural gas should be appropriately bounded. For the 1977 historical comparison the logical bounds are simply the actual 1977 consumption. Hence, in addition to fixing fuel prices and demands at 1977 levels, regional upper bounds on the availability of natural gas have been included in the stand-alone model. This is a reasonable representation of government policy to restrict utility consumption of gas during this period. Also, it is a reflection that the average price of gas, unlike oil, is nowhere near the market price for new gas.

DATA COMPARISON

As mentioned previously, the stand-alone version of the electric utility model is identical to the corresponding module in the overall MEMM system. As such, all the technological parameters, existing capacities, and demand curve character-istics are identical. But since the results of the stand-alone model are to be compared against 1977 EEI statistics, the question arises as to the consistency between the MEMM data base and the EEI statistics. For example, the total U.S. generation capacity used in the 1977 ARC is 539,312 MW (at January 1, 1978). The estimate of total U.S. capacity by EEI for the same date is about 18,000 MW greater, 557,174. The difference is probably due to an inconsistency in the definition of the capacity measured, for example, nameplate or effective. In addition, the weighted overall load factor used in MEMM (for the 1977 ARC) is .598, while EEI reports that in 1977 the overall load factor was .614. (The .598 load factor calculated for MEMM is determined by weighting each region according to the percentage of actual generation in 1977.) These two observations lead to the result that when the stand-alone model is simulated for 1977 there may not be enough capacity to satisfy the reserve margin requirement. These two observations also suggest that some calibration may be necessary in future model developments to ensure that the assumed demand curves are consistent with existing capacity.

Another comparison of actual 1977 data with elements of the MEMM data base may be far more important. One limitation of the electric utility model is that there is no provision for explicit transmission of electricity between regions. The only assumption of this nature is that transmission within a given region is about 90% efficient. Hence, if 100 kWh are generated in a region, then sales are about 90 kWh; that is, the sales to generation ratios are identically equal to the transmission efficiencies. Table A.1 shows that in fact this is not the case. Observe that region 2 is a net importer of electricity, while region 8 is a large exporter of electricity. (For the nation as a whole the 1977 ratio of sales to generation is .918 [52].)

The implication of Table A.1 is that MEMM may have a significant bias in projections of the future. For example, if region 8 is assumed to serve only that demand associated with region 8, then new capacity requirements may be low or nonexistent. Correspondingly, capacity growth for region 2 in 1990 projections would be overstated.

In terms of the 1977 historical comparison, Table A.1 shows that fixing

TABLE A.1.   Regional 1977 Sales-Generation Ratios [52]

	Federal Regions									
	1	2	3	4	5	6	7	8	9	10
Ratio	.95	1.03	.77	.93	.97	.88	.93	.65	1.03	.97

TABLE A.2.   1977 Generation (10^6 kWh/Day)

Federal Region		kWh/Day
1		208.8
2		391.7
3		721.3
4		1223.7
5		1129.3
6		803.9
7		273.6
8		215.9
9		512.4
10		327.3
	Total	5807.9

1977 demand according to *sales* would present a problem to the stand-alone model. There would be too little capacity in region 2 and too much capacity in region 8. On the other hand, if the exogenously fixed demands were stated in terms of generation, then a valid comparison of dispatch strategy can be obtained. The actual regional generation in 1977, according to EEI[52], is given in Table A.2. With the inclusion of the 1977 regional generation scaled by the transmission loss as a surrogate for demand, the specification of the 1977 stand-alone model is complete.

1977 COMPARISON

The actual 1977 generation, by region and fuel type, is shown in Tables A.3 and A.4. These two tables show that the generation mix is quite different across regions. On a national basis, coal represents nearly 50% of the total generation, and hydro accounts for about 1 of every 10 kWh generated.

The hydro percentage for 1977 is somewhat misleading in that 1977 was an extraordinarily dry year. The 1977 hydroelectric generation was the lowest of the

TABLE A.3   Actual 1977 Generation by Plant Type and Region (10^6 kWh/Day)

Plant Type	Region										Total
	1	2	3	4	5	6	7	8	9	10	
Hydro	13.4	69.2	11.9	100.1	9.3	13.0	6.7	50.1	61.6	268.7	603.5
Coal	6.9	58.7	477.9	732.6	886.9	101.3	186.1	154.4	72.0	23.1	2699.9
Oil	117.9	185.6	126.1	170.8	54.4	68.3	10.9	1.8	243.1	1.5	980.4
Gas	.7	2.7	.8	45.7	10.6	607.4	41.6	9.0	113.5	4.4	836.4
Nuclear	69.9	75.5	104.6	174.5	168.1	13.9	28.3	.6	22.2	29.6	687.2
Total	208.8	391.7	721.3	1223.7	1129.3	803.9	273.6	215.9	512.4	327.3	5807.4

TABLE A.4   Actual 1977 Generation Percentages

Plant Type	Region										Total
	1	2	3	4	5	6	7	8	9	10	
Hydro	6.4	17.7	1.6	8.2	.8	1.6	2.4	23.2	12.0	82.1	10.4
Coal	3.3	15.0	66.3	59.9	78.5	12.6	68.0	71.5	14.1	7.1	46.5
Oil	56.5	47.4	17.5	14.0	4.8	8.5	4.0	.8	47.4	.5	16.9
Gas	.3	.7	.1	3.7	.9	75.6	15.2	4.2	22.2	1.3	14.4
Nuclear	33.5	19.3	14.5	14.3	14.9	1.7	10.3	.2	4.3	9.0	11.8

TABLE A.5   Model Results for 1977 (Percent Generation)

Plant Type	Region										Total
	1	2	3	4	5	6	7	8	9	10	
Hydro	7.0	23.8	1.0	7.6	1.2	3.3	1.8	31.1	25.8	100	13.5
Coal	11.0	18.0	64.6	67.7	81.5	15.9	71.8	68.0	6.8	—	48.4
Oil	50.8	32.9	21.1	5.2	.8	2.5	1.6		40.8	—	12.0
Gas	—	.5	5.2	3.1	.6	76.6	13.3	.8	22.3	—	14.0
Nuclear	31.2	24.9	13.3	16.4	15.8	1.7	11.4	—	4.4	—	12.2

previous 10 years. For example, the generation by hydro in 1977 was only 75% of the average of the previous 3 years, 1974, 1975, and 1976. Since 1977 was an off year in terms of hydroelectric generation, it may be expected that the 1977 stand-alone version of the electric utility model would overestimate generation by hydroelectric facilities, since hydroelectric capacity factors are based on long-run averages. This is indeed the case, as is shown in Table A.5. Table A.5 is the model output for the 1977 test year.

In comparing Tables A.4 and A.5, a certain expected pattern is observed. Hydroelectric percentages are, for the most part, uniformly higher in the model (Table A.5) than actual 1977 generation, while the oil percentages are generally lower. Again, this is because 1977 was a poor year for hydro, while the MEMM coefficients are based on the average flow for a year. In addition, coal generation is slightly higher. Not shown in Table A.5 is that the model needed to add about 20,000 MW of new capacity to satisfy the reserve margin requirement. As pointed out previously, this was expected in that the MEMM data base is about 18,000 MW below, on a national basis, the EEI capacity estimate. In addition, the average load factor in MEMM is slightly less than the actual value in 1977.

Taking into account that the model capacity factors for hydroelectric generation are based on an average water year, the model results compare favorably with the actual 1977 generation. Some regions compare better than others; for example, the regions with little hydroelectric, such as regions 1, 3, and 5, are among the best. Regions such as 8, 9, and 10 show a bit more distortion, presumably due to the hydroelectric anomaly.

APPENDIX **B**

BOUNDS ON THE OPTIMAL OUTPUT FOR THE REGULATED FIRM

OVERVIEW

One of the long-standing controversies involving the Averch-Johnson model of profit-maximizing behavior of the regulated firm [3] is whether rate-of-return regulation induces the firm to produce a larger output than the unregulated monopoly. It has been assumed by many that since overcapitalization (of a specific form) is a proven consequence of regulation, then a larger output is a foregone result.

In their 1970 paper, Baumol and Klevorick [8] point out that no such result has ever been proved. According to Baumol and Klevorick [8].

> The invalidity of [larger output for the regulated firm] may be perhaps considered as unfortunate. If it were true, it might be claimed as a virtue of the regulatory process. For, generally, the monopolistic firm's output is taken to be smaller than the level that is socially optimal. . . . Indeed, some authors have defended fair rate of return regulation on the ground that it will have some beneficial effect on output. For example, Alfred E. Kahn recognizes explicitly the input inefficiency such regulation can engender. But, he argues, by inducing the regulated firm to overinvest in capacity and hence to increase its output, fair rate of return helps to reduce—if not overcome—the monopoly's tendency to underinvest and restrict output. The fact that [a larger output] is not true as a general statement weakens somewhat the case of Kahn and others who take a similar position.

Baumol and Klevorick give general conditions under which output increases. These conditions are not easily interpreted. It turns out that the intuitive conjecture of larger output from the regulated firms is true for the case of positive homogeneous production functions of degree k. Hence, in this case the firm subject to a rate-of-return constraint will always produce an output at least as large as the output of the unconstrained monopoly, an output determined where marginal cost equals marginal revenue.

In addition to this lower bound on the optimal output of the regulated firm, there exists an easily derived upper bound that is intimately related to the average cost pricing mechanism of the MEMM utility sector. This upper bound corresponds to the intersection of the "regulated" average cost curve and the demand curve and will be developed first.

DEVELOPMENT OF AN UPPER BOUND

By using the same notation as that developed for (6), a family of programs is defined parametrically in q:

$$f(q) = \min r_1 x_1 + r_2 x_2$$
$$F(x_1, x_2) \geq q$$
$$x_1, x_2 \geq 0$$

That is, $f(q)$ is the least cost method of producing q units. Let $[\bar{x}_1(q), \bar{x}_2(q)]$ be a family of optimal solutions corresponding to an output q. Next, define the *regulated average cost RAC* for an output q as

$$RAC(q) = \frac{s\bar{x}_1(q) + r_2\bar{x}_2(q)}{q}$$

For the case in which F is concave, it follows that $f(q)$ is convex. Hence, the average cost curve $AC(q) = f(q)/q$ is nondecreasing. In this section we make the assumption that $RAC(q)$ is nondecreasing. Let $\bar{q}$ be the (unique) output for which price $p(\bar{q})$ equals $RAC(\bar{q})$. Also, let (q^*, x_1^*, x_2^*) be an optimal solution to the A-J model (6), which means that

$$p(q^*) \leq \frac{sx_1^* + r_2x_2^*}{q^*}$$

It is now shown that $q^* \leq \bar{q}$; that is, the Averch-Johnson output is bounded above by the output associated with the regulated average cost solution.

First, observe that by definition of $f(q^*)$ it follows that

$$r_1\bar{x}_1(q^*) + r_2\bar{x}_2(q^*) \leq r_1 x_1^* + r_2 x_2^* \tag{B.1}$$

Furthermore, it must follow that

$$\bar{x}_1(q^*) \leq x_1^* \tag{B.2}$$

That is, the amount of capital in the least cost solution is bounded above by its counterpart from the Averch-Johnson solution. If (B.2) does not hold, that is, if $\bar{x}_1(q^*) > x_1$, then necessarily $\bar{x}_2(q^*) < x_2^*$, or the optimality of $[\bar{x}_1(q^*), \bar{x}_2(q^*)]$

for $f(q^*)$ would be violated. Hence, if (B.2) is not true, then

$$\frac{\bar{x}_1(q^*)}{\bar{x}_2(q^*)} > \frac{x_1^*}{x_2^*} \tag{B.3}$$

But (B.3) is a contradiction of FACT 2 of Baumol and Klevorick [8] (see page 36), and hence (B.2) is valid. From (B.1) and (B.2) it then follows (since $s > r_1$) that

$$s\bar{x}_1(q^*) + r_2\bar{x}_2(q^*) \leq sx_1^* + r_2x_2^*$$

or

$$\frac{s\bar{x}_1(q^*) + r_2\bar{x}_2(q^*)}{q^*} \leq \frac{sx_1^* + r_2x_2^*}{q^*} \leq p(q^*)$$

Hence,

$$RAC(q^*) \leq p(q^*)$$

Since $p(\bar{q})$ is downward sloping and $RAC(q)$ is nondecreasing, it follows that $q^* \leq \bar{q}$. This result is summarized in the following theorem.

Theorem B.1. Assume $p(q)$ is strictly decreasing and $RAC(q)$ is non-decreasing and let (q^*, x_1^*, x_2^*) be an optimal solution to the Averch-Johnson model (6). If $\bar{q}$ is the (unique) output for which $p(\bar{q}) = RAC(\bar{q})$, then $q^* \leq \bar{q}$.

Theorem B.1 provides the interesting result that the MEMM average cost pricing mechanism provides an output that is an upper bound to the Averch-Johnson output for any choice of $r_1 < s$.

DEVELOPMENT OF A LOWER BOUND

Next, consider the initial conjecture that regulation for the case of positive homogeneous production functions of degree k leads to higher output. [A function $F: R^n \to R$ is said to be positive homogeneous of degree k if $F(\lambda x) = \lambda^k F(x)$ for all $\lambda \geq 0$.] This conjecture is motivated by the graph of Figure B.1 depicting the profit-maximizing monopolist. If the marginal cost curve of the monopolist is given by MC, then the optimal output is q, that is, the point at which marginal revenue is equal to marginal cost. On the other hand, if the marginal cost curve is given by MC', then the output level is $q' > q$. Hence, if the marginal cost curve is everywhere decreased, the monopoly output can only increase.

The key argument to be developed is that the A-J model given by (6) can be recast into an equivalent monopoly problem, a problem with marginal cost curve given by MC'. The following lemma is central to this development.

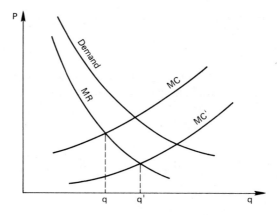

Figure B.1   Profit-maximizing monopolist.

Lemma B.1.   Let $F: R^n \to R$ be concave and positive homogeneous of degree k, and let $c_1, c_2, \in R^n, c_1 \geq c_2$. Define the following for $q \in R_+$:

$$h_1(q) = \min c_1 x$$
$$F(x) \geq q \qquad (\lambda_1)$$
$$x \geq 0$$

and

$$h_2(q) = \min c_2 x$$
$$F(x) \geq q \qquad (\lambda_2)$$
$$x \geq 0$$

where $\lambda_i, i = 1, 2$, are Kuhn-Tucker scalars. Then, assuming $h_i(q)$ is differentiable at q,

$$h_1'(q) \geq h_2'(q)$$

Proof.   According to Greenberg [25], if λ_i^* is an optimal Kuhn-Tucker vector associated with $h_i(q)$, then

$$\frac{1}{k} h_i(q) = \lambda_i^*(q)q$$

since $F(x)$ is positive homogeneous of degree k. Furthermore, since $c_1 \geq c_2$, it follows that

$$h_1(q) \geq h_2(q)$$

for all $q \in R_+$. Hence, $\lambda_1^*(q) \geq \lambda_2^*(q)$. Since it is well known that if $h_i'(q)$ exists, then $h_i'(q) = \lambda_i^*(q)$, the lemma is proved.

The lemma shows that if $c_1 \geq c_2$, then the marginal cost curve associated with $h_2(q)$ will always lie below the marginal cost associated with $h_1(q)$. [Note that $h_i(q)$ are the total cost curves.] With references to Figure B.1, MC is associated with $h_1'(q)$ and MC' with $h_2'(q)$.

Now suppose that $(q^*, x_1^*, x_2^*, \lambda^*, \mu^*)$ represents a pair of dual optimal solutions to (6). It follows that $(q^*, x_1^*, x_2^*, \mu^*)$ must also be optimal for the following:

$$\text{Max } R(q) - r_1 x_1 - r_2 x_2 - \lambda^* [R(q) - sx_1 - r_2 x_2]$$

$$\text{s.t. } q = F(x_1, x_2) \tag{B.5}$$

$$x_1, x_2 \geq 0$$

Rearranging the objective function and then dividing by the constant $1 - \lambda^*$ yield the equivalent problem (B.6); that is, $(q^*, x_1^*, x_2^*, \mu^*)$ is also optimal for the following:

$$\text{Max } R(q) - \frac{r_1 - \lambda^* s}{1 - \lambda^*} x_1 - r_2 x_2$$

$$q = F(x_1, x_2) \tag{B.6}$$

$$x_1, x_2 \geq 0$$

Observe that since $0 \leq \lambda^* < 1$, it follows that

$$\frac{r_1 - \lambda^* s}{1 - \lambda^*} < r_1 \tag{B.7}$$

The interesting conclusion is that the A-J model of (6) can be recast into an equivalent, unconstrained profit-maximizing monopoly (which has a lower cost of capital). This equivalent monopoly formulation exhibits a marginal cost curve of the form MC' that is everywhere less than the marginal cost curve for the monopoly whose cost of capital is r_1 (see Figure B.1).

When $\lambda^* = 0$, (6) [and hence (B.6)] corresponds to an unconstrained monopoly. But if $\lambda^* > 0$, then (B.7) shows that the cost of capital in (B.6) is less than r_1. Since the optimal solution to (B.6) is obtained at the point where marginal cost is equal to marginal revenue, it follows from Lemma B.1 that the optimal output of (B.6) [and hence (6)] is at least as large as the unconstrained monopoly solution, that is, where the cost of capital is r_1. Thus, we have proved the following theorem.

Theorem B.2.   The optimal output for the A-J model (6) with a positive homogeneous production function of degree $k > 0$ is at least as large as an unregulated firm with the same production function.

APPENDIX C

1985 ELECTRIC UTILITIES INPUT DATA FOR FORECASTS BASED ON CURRENT LAW

This appendix provides a listing of the 1985 data input for the electric utility submodel. The 1990 data requirements are analogous and can be found in the 1977 ARC Volume III Appendix.

```
THERE ARE FOUR CATEGORIES OF INPUT DATA ELEMENTS:

LOAD-DURATION-  FACTORS WHICH REPRESENT NONUNIFORM DEMAND REQUIREMENTS
                (I.E. BASE,CYCLING,DAILY PEAK,AND SEASONAL PEAK LOADS);
CAPACITY-       EXISTING AND NEW CAPACITY FOR EACH PLANT TYPE, AND
                MANDATED CONVERSION;
COST-           CAPITAL CHARGES, OPERATION AND MAINTENANCE COSTS,
                SCRUBBING COSTS, AND TRANSMISSION AND DISTRIBUTION COSTS;
PHYSICAL-       HEAT RATES AND VALUES FOR EACH PLANT AND FUEL.

        IN MOST CASES THE DATA VARIES BY DOE REGION. THE DATA ELEMENTS,THEREFORE,
ARE AGGREGATES, COMPUTED FROM A PLANT-BY-PLANT (OR PROJECT-BY-PROJECT) DATABASE.
        TABLE 1 SHOWS REGIONAL COMPOSITION AND CAPACITY FACTORS FOR BASE, CYCLING,
DAILY PEAK, AND SEASONAL PEAK LOADS AS WELL AS THE SYSTEM LOAD FACTORS (I.E. THE
RATIO OF AVERAGE TO PEAK LOAD). THE RESERVE MARGIN IS 20% FOR EACH REGION.
COMPOSITION FACTORS ARE THE FRACTIONS OF ELECTRIC POWER IN EACH LOAD. FOR EXAMPLE,
IN REGION 1 OF ALL ELECTRICITY DEMANDED DURING THE YEAR, 68.7% IS BASE, 24.7% IS
CYCLING, 4.4% IS DAILY PEAK, AND  2.2% IS SEASONAL PEAK. FIGURE 1 SHOWS A
(GENERIC) LOAD-DURATION CURVE WITH THE FOUR LOADS SHOWN AS AREAS UNDER A LINEAR
APPROXIMATION OF THE ACTUAL CURVE.
        GENERATING FACILITIES ARE CLASSIFIED AS BASE, CYCLING, DAILY PEAK OR SEASONAL
PEAK DEPENDING UPON THE ORDER IN WHICH THEY ARE BROUGHT INTO OPERATION AS DEMAND
INCREASES. CAPACITY FACTORS ARE THE FRACTIONS OF TIME A PLANT IS ACTUALLY
OPERATED AND NOT SHUT DOWN FOR REPAIRS OR SCHEDULED MAINTENANCE
OR UNUSED FOR LACK OF SUFFICIENT DEMAND. FOR EXAMPLE, IF AN EXISTING RESIDUAL-
FIRED PLANT IN REGION 1 IS OPERATED IN BASE LOAD FOR A YEAR, THE ACTUAL NUMBER
OF KILOWATT-YEARS OF ELECTRICITY GENERATED, ON THE AVERAGE, WILL BE ITS
CAPACITY (IN KILOWATTS) MULTIPLIED BY ITS CAPACITY FACTOR, IN
THIS CASE .70 . SINCE BASE PLANTS ARE OPERATED ALMOST CONTINUOUSLY WHEN THEY
ARE AVAILABLE, THIS INDICATES THAT THE PLANT WILL BE SHUT DOWN APPROXIMATELY
30% OF THE TIME. FOR THIS SAME PLANT OPERATING IN CYCLING LOAD, THE CAPACITY
FACTOR IS .55 ,REFLECTING THE PERIODS THE PLANT WILL NOT OPERATE BECAUSE THE
DEMAND DOES NOT WARRANT BRINGING IN CYCLING PLANTS AS WELL AS PERIODS WHEN IT IS
FORCED OUT OF SERVICE OR SHUT DOWN FOR MAINTENANCE.
```

TABLE 1:   LOAD-DURATION CURVE DATA FOR 1985

DOE REGION	COMPOSITION FACTORS				SYSTEM LOAD FACTOR
	BASE	CYCLING	DAILY PEAK	SEASONAL PEAK	
NW-ENG.	.687	.247	.044	.022	.590
NY/NJ	.746	.188	.042	.023	.630
MID-ATL	.766	.166	.042	.026	.600
S.-ATL	.770	.158	.043	.029	.600
MIDWEST	.758	.185	.037	.020	.630
S.-WEST	.756	.144	.067	.033	.540
CENTRAL	.749	.156	.063	.033	.550
N-CENTRAL	.783	.167	.026	.024	.600
WEST	.758	.173	.043	.026	.630
N.-WEST	.810	.130	.036	.024	.620

FIGURE 1: LINEAR APPROXIMATION OF A LOAD-DURATION CURVE

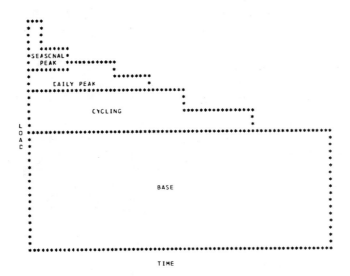

CAPACITY FACTORS FOR DOE REGION 1 (NEW ENGLAND)

	BASE	CYCLING	DAILY PEAK	SEASONAL PEAK
EXISTING PLANTS				
RESIDUAL-FIRED STEAM	.700	.548	.274	−
DISTILLATE-FIRED SIMPLE CYCLE TURBINE	.800	.616	.308	.082
GAS-FIRED STEAM	.700	.548	.274	−
GAS-FIRED TURBINE	.800	.616	.308	.082
DISTILLATE-FIRED COMBINED CYCLE TURBINE	.800	.616	.308	−
BITUMINOUS COAL-FIRED STEAM (WITH SCRUBBING REQUIRED)	.650	.514	.257	−
BITUMINOUS COAL-FIRED STEAM (UNSCRUBBED USING LOW SULFUR COAL)	.650	.514	.257	−
BITUMINOUS COAL-FIRED STEAM (WITH NO SCRUBBING REQUIRED)	.650	.514	.257	−
HYDRO-ELECTRIC (PONDAGE)	.850	.651	.325	.087
HYDRO-ELECTRIC (PUMP STORAGE)	−	−	.325	.087
NUCLEAR	.650	−	−	−
NEW PLANTS				
RESIDUAL-FIRED STEAM	.700	.548	.274	−
DISTILLATE-FIRED SIMPLE CYCLE TURBINE	.800	.616	.308	.082
GAS-FIRED STEAM	.700	.548	.274	−
DISTILLATE-FIRED COMBINED CYCLE TURBINE	.800	.616	.308	−
BITUMINOUS COAL-FIRED STEAM (WITH SCRUBBING REQUIRED)	.650	.514	.257	−
BITUMINOUS COAL-FIRED STEAM (UNSCRUBBED USING LOW SULFUR COAL)	.650	.514	.257	−
SUB-BITUMINOUS COAL-FIRED STEAM	.650	.514	.257	−
HYDRO-ELECTRIC (PONDAGE)	.850	.651	.325	.087
HYDRO-ELECTRIC (PUMP STORAGE)	.850	.651	.325	.087
NUCLEAR	.650	−	−	−

CAPACITY FACTORS FOR DOE REGION 2   (NEW YORK AND NEW JERSEY)

	BASE	CYCLING	DAILY PEAK	SEASONAL PEAK
EXISTING PLANTS				
RESIDUAL-FIRED STEAM	.700	.548	.274	–
DISTILLATE-FIRED SIMPLE CYCLE TURBINE	.800	.616	.308	.082
GAS-FIRED STEAM	.700	.548	.274	–
GAS-FIRED TURBINE	.800	.616	.308	.082
DISTILLATE-FIRED COMBINED CYCLE TURBINE	.800	.616	.308	–
BITUMINOUS COAL-FIRED STEAM (WITH SCRUBBING REQUIRED)	.650	.514	.257	–
BITUMINOUS COAL-FIRED STEAM (UNSCRUBBED USING LOW SULFUR COAL)	.650	.514	.257	–
BITUMINOUS COAL-FIRED STEAM (WITH NO SCRUBBING REQUIRED)	.650	.514	.257	–
HYDRO-ELECTRIC (PONDAGE)	.850	.651	.325	.087
HYDRO-ELECTRIC (PUMP STORAGE)	–	–	.325	.087
NUCLEAR	.650	–	–	–
NEW PLANTS				
RESIDUAL-FIRED STEAM	.700	.548	.274	–
DISTILLATE-FIRED SIMPLE CYCLE TURBINE	.800	.616	.308	.082
GAS-FIRED STEAM	.700	.548	.274	–
DISTILLATE-FIRED COMBINED CYCLE TURBINE	.800	.616	.308	–
BITUMINOUS COAL-FIRED STEAM (WITH SCRUBBING REQUIRED)	.650	.514	.257	–
BITUMINOUS COAL-FIRED STEAM (UNSCRUBBED USING LOW SULFUR COAL)	.650	.514	.257	–
SUB-BITUMINOUS COAL-FIRED STEAM	.650	.514	.257	–
HYDRO-ELECTRIC (PONDAGE)	.850	.651	.325	.087
HYDRO-ELECTRIC (PUMP STORAGE)	.850	.651	.325	.087
NUCLEAR	.650	–	–	–

CAPACITY FACTORS FOR DOE REGION 3   (MID-ATLANTIC)

	BASE	CYCLING	DAILY PEAK	SEASONAL PEAK
EXISTING PLANTS				
RESIDUAL-FIRED STEAM	.700	.548	.274	–
DISTILLATE-FIRED SIMPLE CYCLE TURBINE	.800	.616	.308	.082
GAS-FIRED STEAM	.700	.548	.274	–
GAS-FIRED TURBINE	.800	.616	.308	.082
DISTILLATE-FIRED COMBINED CYCLE TURBINE	.800	.616	.308	–
BITUMINOUS COAL-FIRED STEAM (WITH SCRUBBING REQUIRED)	.650	.514	.257	–
BITUMINOUS COAL-FIRED STEAM (UNSCRUBBED USING LOW SULFUR COAL)	.650	.514	.257	–
BITUMINOUS COAL-FIRED STEAM (WITH NO SCRUBBING REQUIRED)	.650	.514	.257	–
HYDRO-ELECTRIC (PONDAGE)	.850	.651	.325	.087
HYDRO-ELECTRIC (PUMP STORAGE)	–	–	.325	.087
NUCLEAR	.650	–	–	–
NEW PLANTS				
RESIDUAL-FIRED STEAM	.700	.548	.274	–
DISTILLATE-FIRED SIMPLE CYCLE TURBINE	.800	.616	.308	.082
GAS-FIRED STEAM	.700	.548	.274	–
DISTILLATE-FIRED COMBINED CYCLE TURBINE	.800	.616	.308	–
BITUMINOUS COAL-FIRED STEAM (WITH SCRUBBING REQUIRED)	.650	.514	.257	–
BITUMINOUS COAL-FIRED STEAM (UNSCRUBBED USING LOW SULFUR COAL)	.650	.514	.257	–
SUB-BITUMINOUS COAL-FIRED STEAM	.650	.514	.257	–
HYDRO-ELECTRIC (PONDAGE)	.850	.651	.325	.087
HYDRO-ELECTRIC (PUMP STORAGE)	.850	.651	.325	.087
NUCLEAR	.650	–	–	–

CAPACITY FACTORS FOR DOE REGION 4 (SOUTH ATLANTIC)

	BASE	CYCLING	DAILY PEAK	SEASONAL PEAK
EXISTING PLANTS				
RESIDUAL-FIRED STEAM	.700	.548	.274	-
DISTILLATE-FIRED SIMPLE CYCLE TURBINE	.800	.616	.308	.082
GAS-FIRED STEAM	.700	.548	.274	-
GAS-FIRED TURBINE	.800	.616	.308	.082
DISTILLATE-FIRED COMBINED CYCLE TURBINE	.800	.616	.308	-
BITUMINOUS COAL-FIRED STEAM (WITH SCRUBBING REQUIRED)	.650	.514	.257	-
BITUMINOUS COAL-FIRED STEAM (UNSCRUBBED USING LOW SULFUR COAL)	.650	.514	.257	-
BITUMINOUS COAL-FIRED STEAM (WITH NO SCRUBBING REQUIRED)	.650	.514	.257	-
HYDRO-ELECTRIC (PONDAGE)	.850	.651	.325	.087
HYDRO-ELECTRIC (PUMP STORAGE)	-	-	.325	.087
NUCLEAR	.650	-	-	-
NEW PLANTS				
RESIDUAL-FIRED STEAM	.700	.548	.274	-
DISTILLATE-FIRED SIMPLE CYCLE TURBINE	.800	.616	.308	.082
GAS-FIRED STEAM	.700	.548	.274	-
DISTILLATE-FIRED COMBINED CYCLE TURBINE	.800	.616	.308	-
BITUMINOUS COAL-FIRED STEAM (WITH SCRUBBING REQUIRED)	.650	.514	.257	-
BITUMINOUS COAL-FIRED STEAM (UNSCRUBBED USING LOW SULFUR COAL)	.650	.514	.257	-
SUB-BITUMINOUS COAL-FIRED STEAM	.650	.514	.257	-
HYDRO-ELECTRIC (PONDAGE)	.850	.651	.325	.097
HYDRO-ELECTRIC (PUMP STORAGE)	.850	.651	.325	.087
NUCLEAR	.650	-	-	-

CAPACITY FACTORS FOR DOE REGION 5 (MIDWEST)

	BASE	CYCLING	DAILY PEAK	SEASONAL PEAK
EXISTING PLANTS				
RESIDUAL-FIRED STEAM	.700	.548	.274	-
DISTILLATE-FIRED SIMPLE CYCLE TURBINE	.800	.616	.308	.082
GAS-FIRED STEAM	.700	.548	.274	-
GAS-FIRED TURBINE	.800	.616	.308	.082
DISTILLATE-FIRED COMBINED CYCLE TURBINE	.800	.616	.308	-
BITUMINOUS COAL-FIRED STEAM (WITH SCRUBBING REQUIRED)	.650	.514	.257	-
BITUMINOUS COAL-FIRED STEAM (UNSCRUBBED USING LOW SULFUR COAL)	.650	.514	.257	-
BITUMINOUS COAL-FIRED STEAM (WITH NO SCRUBBING REQUIRED)	.650	.514	.257	-
SUB-BITUMINOUS COAL-FIRED STEAM	.650	.514	.257	-
LIGNITE COAL-FIRED STEAM	.650	.514	.257	-
HYDRO-ELECTRIC (PONDAGE)	.850	.651	.325	.087
HYDRO-ELECTRIC (PUMP STORAGE)	-	-	.325	.087
NUCLEAR	.650	-	-	-
NEW PLANTS				
RESIDUAL-FIRED STEAM	.700	.548	.274	-
DISTILLATE-FIRED SIMPLE CYCLE TURBINE	.800	.616	.308	.082
GAS-FIRED STEAM	.700	.548	.274	-
DISTILLATE-FIRED COMBINED CYCLE TURBINE	.800	.616	.308	-
BITUMINOUS COAL-FIRED STEAM (WITH SCRUBBING REQUIRED)	.650	.514	.257	-
BITUMINOUS COAL-FIRED STEAM (UNSCRUBBED USING LOW SULFUR COAL)	.650	.514	.257	-
SUB-BITUMINOUS COAL-FIRED STEAM	.650	.514	.257	-
LIGNITE COAL-FIRED STEAM	.650	.514	.257	-
HYDRO-ELECTRIC (PONDAGE)	.850	.651	.325	.087
HYDRO-ELECTRIC (PUMP STORAGE)	.850	.651	.325	.087
NUCLEAR	.650	-	-	-

CAPACITY FACTORS FOR DOE REGION 6   (SOUTHWEST)

	BASE	CYCLING	DAILY PEAK	SEASONAL PEAK
EXISTING PLANTS				
RESIDUAL-FIRED STEAM	.700	.548	.274	-
DISTILLATE-FIRED SIMPLE CYCLE TURBINE	.800	.616	.308	.082
GAS-FIRED STEAM	.700	.548	.274	-
GAS-FIRED TURBINE	.800	.616	.308	.082
DISTILLATE-FIRED COMBINED CYCLE TURBINE	.800	.616	.308	-
SUB-BITUMINOUS COAL-FIRED STEAM	.650	.514	.257	-
LIGNITE COAL-FIRED STEAM	.650	.514	.257	-
HYDRO-ELECTRIC (PONDAGE)	.850	.651	.325	.087
HYDRO-ELECTRIC (PUMP STORAGE)	-	-	.325	.087
NUCLEAR	.650	-	-	-
NEW PLANTS				
RESIDUAL-FIRED STEAM	.700	.548	.274	-
DISTILLATE-FIRED SIMPLE CYCLE TURBINE	.800	.616	.308	.082
GAS-FIRED STEAM	.700	.548	.274	-
DISTILLATE-FIRED COMBINED CYCLE TURBINE	.800	.616	.308	-
BITUMINOUS COAL-FIRED STEAM (WITH SCRUBBING REQUIRED)	.650	.514	.257	-
BITUMINOUS COAL-FIRED STEAM (UNSCRUBBED USING LOW SULFUR COAL)	.650	.514	.257	-
SUB-BITUMINOUS COAL-FIRED STEAM	.650	.514	.257	-
LIGNITE COAL-FIRED STEAM	.650	.514	.257	-
HYDRO-ELECTRIC (PONDAGE)	.850	.651	.325	.087
HYDRO-ELECTRIC (PUMP STORAGE)	.850	.651	.325	.087
NUCLEAR	.650	-	-	-

CAPACITY FACTORS FOR DOE REGION 7   (CENTRAL)

	BASE	CYCLING	DAILY PEAK	SEASONAL PEAK
EXISTING PLANTS				
RESIDUAL-FIRED STEAM	.700	.548	.274	-
DISTILLATE-FIRED SIMPLE CYCLE TURBINE	.800	.616	.308	.082
GAS-FIRED STEAM	.700	.548	.274	-
GAS-FIRED TURBINE	.800	.616	.308	.082
DISTILLATE-FIRED COMBINED CYCLE TURBINE	.800	.616	.308	-
BITUMINOUS COAL-FIRED STEAM (WITH SCRUBBING REQUIRED)	.650	.514	.257	-
BITUMINOUS COAL-FIRED STEAM (UNSCRUBBED USING LOW SULFUR COAL)	.650	.514	.257	-
BITUMINOUS COAL-FIRED STEAM (WITH NO SCRUBBING REQUIRED)	.650	.514	.257	-
SUB-BITUMINOUS COAL-FIRED STEAM	.650	.514	.257	-
HYDRO-ELECTRIC (PONDAGE)	.850	.651	.325	.087
HYDRO-ELECTRIC (PUMP STORAGE)	-	-	.325	.087
NUCLEAR	.650	-	-	-
NEW PLANTS				
RESIDUAL-FIRED STEAM	.700	.548	.274	-
DISTILLATE-FIRED SIMPLE CYCLE TURBINE	.800	.616	.308	.082
GAS-FIRED STEAM	.700	.548	.274	-
DISTILLATE-FIRED COMBINED CYCLE TURBINE	.800	.616	.308	-
BITUMINOUS COAL-FIRED STEAM (WITH SCRUBBING REQUIRED)	.650	.514	.257	-
BITUMINOUS COAL-FIRED STEAM (UNSCRUBBED USING LOW SULFUR COAL)	.650	.514	.257	-
SUB-BITUMINOUS COAL-FIRED STEAM	.650	.514	.257	-
HYDRO-ELECTRIC (PONDAGE)	.850	.651	.325	.087
HYDRO-ELECTRIC (PUMP STORAGE)	.850	.651	.325	.087
NUCLEAR	.650	-	-	-

CAPACITY FACTORS FOR DOE REGION 8 (NORTH CENTRAL)

	BASE	CYCLING	DAILY PEAK	SEASONAL PEAK
EXISTING PLANTS				
RESIDUAL-FIRED STEAM	.700	.548	.274	–
DISTILLATE-FIRED SIMPLE CYCLE TURBINE	.800	.616	.308	.082
GAS-FIRED STEAM	.700	.548	.274	–
GAS-FIRED TURBINE	.800	.616	.308	.082
BITUMINOUS COAL-FIRED STEAM	.650	.514	.257	–
(WITH SCRUBBING REQUIRED)				
BITUMINOUS COAL-FIRED STEAM	.650	.514	.257	–
(UNSCRUBBED USING LOW SULFUR COAL)				
BITUMINOUS COAL-FIRED STEAM	.650	.514	.257	–
(WITH NO SCRUBBING REQUIRED)				
SUB-BITUMINOUS COAL-FIRED STEAM	.650	.514	.257	–
LIGNITE COAL-FIRED STEAM	.650	.514	.257	–
HYDRO-ELECTRIC (PONDAGE)	.850	.651	.325	.087
HYDRO-ELECTRIC (PUMP STORAGE)	–	–	.325	.087
NUCLEAR	.650	–	–	–
NEW PLANTS				
RESIDUAL-FIRED STEAM	.700	.548	.274	–
DISTILLATE-FIRED SIMPLE CYCLE TURBINE	.800	.616	.308	.082
GAS-FIRED STEAM	.700	.548	.274	–
DISTILLATE-FIRED COMBINED CYCLE TURBINE	.800	.616	.308	–
BITUMINOUS COAL-FIRED STEAM	.650	.514	.257	–
(WITH SCRUBBING REQUIRED)				
BITUMINOUS COAL-FIRED STEAM	.650	.514	.257	–
(UNSCRUBBED USING LOW SULFUR COAL)				
SUB-BITUMINOUS COAL-FIRED STEAM	.650	.514	.257	–
LIGNITE COAL-FIRED STEAM	.650	.514	.257	–
HYDRO-ELECTRIC (PONDAGE)	.850	.651	.325	.087
HYDRO-ELECTRIC (PUMP STORAGE)	.850	.651	.325	.087
NUCLEAR	.650	–	–	–

CAPACITY FACTORS FOR DOE REGION 9 (WEST)

	BASE	CYCLING	DAILY PEAK	SEASONAL PEAK
EXISTING PLANTS				
RESIDUAL-FIRED STEAM	.700	.548	.274	–
DISTILLATE-FIRED SIMPLE CYCLE TURBINE	.800	.616	.308	.082
GAS-FIRED STEAM	.700	.548	.274	–
GAS-FIRED TURBINE	.800	.616	.308	.082
DISTILLATE-FIRED COMBINED CYCLE TURBINE	.800	.616	.308	–
BITUMINOUS COAL-FIRED STEAM	.650	.514	.257	–
(WITH SCRUBBING REQUIRED)				
BITUMINOUS COAL-FIRED STEAM	.650	.514	.257	–
(UNSCRUBBED USING LOW SULFUR COAL)				
BITUMINOUS COAL-FIRED STEAM	.650	.514	.257	–
(WITH NO SCRUBBING REQUIRED)				
HYDRO-ELECTRIC (PONDAGE)	.850	.651	.325	.087
HYDRO-ELECTRIC (PUMP STORAGE)	–	–	.325	.087
NUCLEAR	.650	–	–	–
NEW PLANTS				
RESIDUAL-FIRED STEAM	.700	.548	.274	–
DISTILLATE-FIRED SIMPLE CYCLE TURBINE	.800	.616	.308	.082
GAS-FIRED STEAM	.700	.548	.274	–
DISTILLATE-FIRED COMBINED CYCLE TURBINE	.800	.616	.308	–
BITUMINOUS COAL-FIRED STEAM	.650	.514	.257	–
(WITH SCRUBBING REQUIRED)				
BITUMINOUS COAL-FIRED STEAM	.650	.514	.257	–
(UNSCRUBBED USING LOW SULFUR COAL)				
SUB-BITUMINOUS COAL-FIRED STEAM	.650	.514	.257	–
HYDRO-ELECTRIC (PONDAGE)	.850	.651	.325	.087
HYDRO-ELECTRIC (PUMP STORAGE)	.850	.651	.325	.087
NUCLEAR	.650	–	–	–

CAPACITY FACTORS FOR DOE REGION 10 (NORTHWEST)

	BASE	CYCLING	DAILY PEAK	SEASONAL PEAK
EXISTING PLANTS				
RESIDUAL-FIRED STEAM	.700	.548	.274	-
DISTILLATE-FIRED SIMPLE CYCLE TURBINE	.800	.616	.308	.082
GAS-FIRED STEAM	.700	.548	.274	-
GAS-FIRED TURBINE	.800	.616	.308	.082
DISTILLATE-FIRED COMBINED CYCLE TURBINE	.800	.616	.308	-
SUB-BITUMINOUS COAL-FIRED STEAM	.650	.514	.257	-
HYDRO-ELECTRIC (PONDAGE)	.850	.651	.325	.087
HYDRO-ELECTRIC (PUMP STORAGE)	-	-	.325	.087
NUCLEAR	.650	-	-	-
NEW PLANTS				
RESIDUAL-FIRED STEAM	.700	.548	.274	-
DISTILLATE-FIRED SIMPLE CYCLE TURBINE	.800	.616	.308	.082
GAS-FIRED STEAM	.700	.548	.274	-
DISTILLATE-FIRED COMBINED CYCLE TURBINE	.800	.616	.308	-
BITUMINOUS COAL-FIRED STEAM (WITH SCRUBBING REQUIRED)	.650	.514	.257	-
BITUMINOUS COAL-FIRED STEAM (UNSCRUBBED USING LOW SULFUR COAL)	.650	.514	.257	-
SUB-BITUMINOUS COAL-FIRED STEAM	.650	.514	.257	-
HYDRO-ELECTRIC (PONDAGE)	.850	.651	.325	.087
HYDRO-ELECTRIC (PUMP STORAGE)	.850	.651	.325	.087
NUCLEAR	.650	-	-	-

TABLE 2 BELOW SHOWS EXISTING CAPACITY FOR EACH PLANT TYPE IN EACH DOE REGION. TABLE 3 SHOWS THE EXISTING CAPACITIES WHICH MAY BE CONVERTED TO ALTERNATE FUEL TYPES AS WELL AS THE MANDATED CONVERSIONS ACCORDING TO THE ENERGY SUPPLY AND ENVIRONMENTAL COORDINATION ACT (ESECA) AS OF JUNE 30, 1977.

TABLE 2: EXISTING CAPACITY (MEGAWATTS)*

PLANT TYPE	1	2	3	4	DOE REGION 5	6	7	8	9	10	TOTAL
RESIDUAL-FIRED STEAM	10286	21489	13690	16117	10122	3676	1150	394	25074	204	102202
DISTILLATE-FIRED SIMPLE CYCLE TURBINE	1276	8583	4473	7900	6534	543	3373	936	3567	960	38145
DISTILLATE-FIRED COMBINED CYCLE TURBINE	170	931	203	619	217	1112	70	-	1219	612	5153
GAS-FIRED STEAM	-	50	-	2981	1035	55052	4957	248	1053	35	65411
GAS-FIRED TURBINE	-	130	414	2418	1110	1806	700	44	59	50	6731
BITUMINOUS COAL-FIRED STEAM (UNSCRUBBED USING LOW SULFUR COAL)	1024	1624		3589	12802		706	1170	1772		24288
BITUMINOUS COAL-FIRED STEAM (WITH SCRUBBING REQUIRED)	-	-	3263	2370	1470	-	965	-	490	-	6957
BITUMINOUS COAL-FIRED STEAM (WITH NO SCRUBBING REQUIRED)	485	2950	26908	48731	40296	-	9486	2215	1616	-	132687
SUB-BITUMINOUS COAL-FIRED STEAM	-	-	-	-	13385	3338	3248	4554	-	1300	25825
LIGNITE COAL-FIRED STEAM	-	-	-	-	141	4857	-	2039	-	-	7037
HYDRO-ELECTRIC (PONDAGE)	1303	5187	1101	10445	1436	2004	636	5390	10128	23861	61491
HYDRO-ELECTRIC (PUMP STORAGE)	1607	1629	1432	921	1979	299	408	334	1646	100	10355
NUCLEAR	4199	6132	6112	12838	11391	850	2010	-	1411	1130	46073
REGIONAL AND NATIONAL TOTALS	20350	48705	57596	108929	101918	73537	27709	17324	48035	28252	532355

*AS OF 1/1/78

TABLE 3: EXISTING CAPACITIES WHICH MAY BE CONVERTED TO BURN ALTERNATE FUEL TYPES

PLANT TYPE	1	2	3	4	DOE REGION 5	6	7	8	9	10	TOTALS
RESIDUAL-FIRED STEAM PLANTS WHICH * MUST BE CONVERTED TO COAL	2488	6822	4063	1794	656	-	46	68	-	-	15937
GAS-FIRED STEAM PLANTS WHICH CAN BE CONVERTED TO RESIDUAL	-	-	-	1764	68	45968	2700	168	744	35	51447
RESIDUAL-FIRED STEAM PLANTS WHICH CAN BE CONVERTED TO GAS	185	4539	443	6513	2288	1578	231	123	22936	53	38889
GAS-FIRED TURBINES WHICH CAN BE CONVERTED TO DISTILLATE	-	-	-	2396	628	327	531	31	59	50	4022
DISTILLATE-FIRED TURBINES WHICH CAN BE CONVERTED TO GAS	291	3208	386	2851	2610	106	616	314	2399	256	13037
GAS-FIRED STEAM PLANTS WHICH MUST BE CONVERTED TO COAL	-	-	-	-	-	-	685	-	-	-	685
REGIONAL AND NATIONAL TOTALS	2964	14569	4892	15318	6250	47979	4809	704	26138	394	124017

*MANDATED CONVERSIONS ACCORDING TO THE ENERGY SUPPLY AND ENVIRONMENTAL COORDINATION ACT (ESECA) AS OF JUNE 30, 1977.

TABLE 4 SHOWS RETIREMENT RATES FOR EXISTING FOSSIL FUEL FIRED FACILITIES IN 1990. FOSSIL FUEL PLANTSCOAL, OIL AND GAS FIRED FACILITIES.

TABLE 4: RETIREMENT RATES FOR FOSSIL FUEL FIRED PLANTS (PERCENT)

YEAR	DOE REGION									
	1	2	3	4	5	6	7	8	9	10
1990	.023	.047	.016	.011	.014	.024	.028	.001	.039	.308

TABLES 5 AND 6 SHOW COMMITTED AND DEFERRABLE CAPACITIES FOR COAL, RESIDUAL, DISTILLATE, NATURAL GAS AND NUCLEAR PLANTS. TABLE 7 SHOWS BUILD LIMITS FOR NUCLEAR, COAL, RESIDUAL AND HYDRO-ELECTRIC PLANTS. COMMITTED PROJECTS HAVE ESSENTIALLY ALL OF THE CAPITAL SUNK AND CONSTRUCTION IS NEARLY COMPLETED. DEFERRABLE PROJECTS HAVE SUNK APPROXIMATELY 10% OF THEIR CAPITAL REQUIREMENTS AND GROUND HAS BEEN BROKEN; HOWEVER THEY MAY BE DEFERRED UNTIL AFTER THE FORECAST YEAR IF IT IS ECONOMICAL TO DO SO. NEW PROJECTS HAVE NO CAPITAL SUNK, BUT THEY MAY HAVE ENTERED THE PLANNING STAGE. SINCE ALL NUCLEAR PLANTS THAT WOULD BE COMPLETE BY 1985 HAVE ALREADY BEEN REGISTERED WITH THE U.S. NUCLEAR REGULATORY COMMISSION, THERE ARE ASSOCIATED LIMITS IN THE MODEL. THE LIMITS FOR NUCLEAR CAPACITY IN 1990, FOR COAL-FIRED STEAM IN 1985, FOR RESIDUAL-FIRED STEAM AND HYDRO-ELECTRIC IN 1985 AND 1990 ARE ESTIMATED BOUNDS ON THE GROWTH OF NUCLEAR, COAL-FIRED STEAM, RESIDUAL-FIRED STEAM AND HYDRO-ELECTRIC CAPACITY, RESPECTIVELY. ALL OTHER PLANT TYPES HAVE NO LIMITS FOR 1985 AND 1990 BECAUSE THOSE YEARS ARE BEYOND THEIR PLANNING CYCLES. EXCEPT, NO NEW GAS STEAM OR GAS TURBINE PLANTS MAY BE BUILT, OTHER THAN THE COMMITTED PLANTS SHOWN IN TABLE 5.

TABLE 5: COMMITTED* CAPACITY FOR 1990
(MEGAWATTS)

PLANT TYPE	DOE REGION										TOTALS
	1	2	3	4	5	6	7	8	9	10	
NUCLEAR	3524	8253	10121	33315	20114	10664	3700	330	8340	4914	103275
RESIDUAL-FIRED STEAM	600	850	–	688	2340	480	–	–	292	198	5448
BITUMINOUS COAL-FIRED STEAM (WITHOUT SCRUBBERS)	–	–	400	1532	1892	–	1250	600	1200	–	6874
BITUMINOUS COAL-FIRED STEAM (WITH SCRUBBERS)	–	–	2077	2905	4853	–	–	–	–	–	9835
SUB-BITUMINOUS COAL-FIRED STEAM	–	–	–	897	4541	2066	2090	–	–	–	9594
LIGNITE COAL-FIRED STEAM	–	–	–	–	641	2685	–	339	–	–	3665
DISTILLATE-FIRED SIMPLE CYCLE TURBINE	6	–	200	300	405	239	778	246	198	–	2372
DISTILLATE-FIRED COMBINED CYCLE TURBINE	230	–	–	–	–	–	–	809	–	–	1039
GAS-FIRED STEAM	–	–	–	–	–	550	–	–	–	–	550
REGIONAL AND NATIONAL TOTALS	4360	9103	12798	38740	31142	19159	7794	3605	10839	5112	142652

*ALL CAPITAL SUNK AND CONSTRUCTION NEARLY COMPLETED

TABLE 6: DEFERRABLE* CAPACITY FOR 1990
(MEGAWATTS)

PLANT TYPE	DOE REGION										TOTALS
	1	2	3	4	5	6	7	8	9	10	
NUCLEAR	–	2134	–	900	–	–	–	–	–	–	3034
BITUMINOUS COAL-FIRED STEAM	–	–	1300	2710	2143	1100	1275	400	700	–	9628
SUB-BITUMINOUS COAL-FIRED STEAM	–	–	–	–	580	6346	1910	2780	–	500	12116
LIGNITE COAL-FIRED STEAM	–	–	–	–	556	1978	–	294	–	–	2828
REGIONAL AND NATIONAL TOTALS	–	2134	1300	3610	3279	9424	3185	3474	700	500	27606

*APPROXIMATELY 10% OF CAPITAL SUNK, GROUND HAS BEEN BROKEN AND PLANT SCHEDULED TO OPERATE BY 1990

TABLE 7: NEW PLANT CAPACITY LIMITS (1990)
(MEGAWATTS)

PLANT TYPE	DOE REGION										TOTALS
	1	2	3	4	5	6	7	8	9	10	
NUCLEAR	2344	1150	181	–	3784	2113	250	–	974	–	14557
RESIDUAL-FIRED STEAM	–	–	610	–	–	–	–	–	–	864	1474
LIGNITE COAL-FIRED STEAM	–	–	–	–	1703	–	–	–	–	–	1703
HYDRO-ELECTRIC (PONDAGE)	384	32	287	1180	150	174	42	1349	1416	9476	14490
HYDRO-ELECTRIC (PUMP STORAGE)	36	2350	6054	4415	–	446	1199	200	2961	650	18311
REGIONAL AND NATIONAL TOTALS	2764	3532	7132	5595	5637	2733	1491	1549	5351	14751	50535

TABLE 8 SHOWS THE OPERATION AND MAINTENANCE COSTS FOR EACH PLANT TYPE.
TABLE 9 SHOWS REVENUE REQUIREMENTS FOR EXISTING EQUIPMENT. TABLE 10
SHOWS THE CAPITAL COSTS FOR NEW PLANTS IN 1990. TABLES 11 AND 12 SHOW ASSOCIATED
CHARGE FACTORS. THE REVENUE REQUIREMENT CHARGE FACTOR IS USED IN THE RATE BASE
COMPUTATION (WHICH IS AVERAGE, RATHER THAN MARGINAL, COST). THE INVESTMENT CHARGE
FACTOR IS USED IN DETERMINING THE DECISION OF WHICH PLANT IS TO BE BUILT IF MORE
CAPACITY IS REQUIRED TO MEET DEMAND. THE REVENUE REQUIREMENT CHARGE FACTORS
ARE REPORTED BY REGION, BECAUSE THESE CHARGE FACTORS ARE BASED ON AVERAGE
COSTS OF PRODUCING ELECTRICITY, RATHER THAN THE MARGINAL COSTS FOR
ANY PARTICULAR PLANT TYPE. ON THE OTHER HAND, THE INVESTMENT CHARGE
IS REPORTED BY PLANT TYPE BECAUSE OF THE DIFFERENT INCOME TAX TREATMENT
EACH PLANT TYPE RECEIVES UNDER THE IRS CODE. TABLE 13 SHOWS TRANSMISSION
AND DISTRIBUTION COSTS AS WELL AS EFFICIENCY RATES (E.G. IN REGION 1 FOR EVERY
KILOWATT GENERATED, ONLY .914 KILOWATTS IS DISTRIBUTED.)

TABLE 8: OPERATION AND MAINTENANCE COSTS
(1975 MILLS PER KILOWATT HOUR)

PLANT TYPE	O&M COST
RESIDUAL-FIRED STEAM	.90
BITUMINOUS COAL * (WITH SCRUBBER)	2.80
(WITHOUT SCRUBBER)	1.10
SUB-BITUMINOUS COAL** (WITH SCRUBBER)	2.00
(WITHOUT SCRUBBER)	1.10
LIGNITE COAL*** (WITH SCRUBBER)	2.00
(WITHOUT SCRUBBER)	1.10
DISTILLATE-FIRED SIMPLE CYCLE	2.75
DISTILLATE-FIRED COMBINED CYCLE	1.25
GAS-FIRED TURBINE	2.75
GAS-FIRED STEAM	.50
HYDRO-ELECTRIC (PONDAGE)	.70
HYDRO-ELECTRIC (PUMP STORAGE)	.70
NUCLEAR	1.65

* BITUMINOUS PLANTS MAY BE SCRUBBED OR UNSCRUBBED
  EXCEPT FOR NEW PLANTS IN DOE REGIONS 8, 9 AND 10
  WHICH MUST BE SCRUBBED AND USE LOW SULFUR COAL
** SUB-BITUMINOUS PLANTS ARE ASSUMED TO BE UNSCRUBBED
   EXCEPT FOR NEW PLANTS IN DOE REGIONS 8, 9 AND 10
   WHICH ARE ASSUMED TO BE SCRUBBED
*** NEW LIGNITE PLANTS ARE ASSUMED TO BE SCRUBBED;
    WHILE EXISTING PLANTS ARE ASSUMED TO BE UNSCRUBBED

TABLE 9: REVENUE REQUIREMENTS IN 1990
FOR EXISTING ASSETS

DOE REGION	REVENUE REQUIREMENTS (MILLIONS OF 1975 $)
1	601
2	1596
3	1685
4	1896
5	2326
6	1061
7	590
8	369
9	1072
10	493

TABLE 10: CAPITAL COSTS OF NEW PLANTS IN 1990
(1975 DOLLARS PER KILOWATT)

PLANT TYPE	DOE REGION									
	1	2	3	4	5	6	7	8	9	10
RESIDUAL-FIRED STEAM	415	438	393	373	409	375	406	391	522	403
BITUMINOUS COAL(WITH SCRUBBER) *	556	588	529	501	549	503	545	524	567	541
BITUMINOUS COAL(WITHOUT SCRUBBER) *	447	473	424	402	442	405	438	524	567	541
SUB-BITUMINOUS COAL *	485	513	461	436	479	439	476	560	605	578
LIGNITE COAL *	591	591	591	591	591	591	591	591	591	591
DISTILLATE-FIRED SIMPLE CYCLE	163	163	163	163	163	163	163	163	163	163
DISTILLATE-FIRED COMBINED CYCLE	312	312	312	312	312	312	312	312	312	312
GAS-FIRED STEAM	350	350	350	285	315	285	315	330	325	325
HYDRO-ELECTRIC (PONDAGE)	400	340	470	420	450	520	490	330	620	220
HYDRO-ELECTRIC (PUMP STORAGE)	400	340	470	420	450	520	490	330	620	220
NUCLEAR (NEW)	695	810	695	570	695	635	670	-	705	790
NUCLEAR (DEFERRABLE)	-	585	-	599	-	-	-	-	-	-

* CAPITAL COST OF DEFFERRABLE COAL PLANTS IS .90 OF NEW PLANT COSTS

NOTE: RETROFITTING AN EXISTING BITUMINOUS COAL PLANT USING HIGH
SULFUR COAL IN BASELOAD COSTS $131 PER KILOWATT

TABLE 11: CAPITAL CHARGE RATES (PERCENT) FOR
          REVENUE REQUIREMENTS

DOE REGION	CAPITAL CHARGE RATES FOR REVENUE REQUIREMENTS
	1990
1	14.0
2	17.4
3	12.7
4	10.0
5	13.3
6	11.9
7	12.9
8	9.9
9	11.7
10	6.3

TABLE 12: CAPITAL CHARGE RATES FOR INVESTMENT
          DECISIONS (ANNUAL PERCENT)

PLANT TYPE	CAPITAL CHARGE RATE FOR INVESTMENT DECISIONS
RESIDUAL-FIRED STEAM	11.4
BITUMINOUS COAL-FIRED STEAM (WITH SCRUBBER)	12.5
BITUMINOUS COAL-FIRED STEAM (WITHOUT SCRUBBER)	11.4
DISTILLATE-FIRED SIMPLE CYCLE TURBINE	10.5
DISTILLATE-FIRED COMBINED CYCLE TURBINE	10.9
GAS-FIRED STEAM	11.4
HYDRO	10.2
SUB-BITUMINOUS COAL-FIRED STEAM	11.4
LIGNITE COAL-FIRED STEAM	11.4
NUCLEAR	11.4

TABLE 13: TRANSMISSION AND DISTRIBUTION DATA

DOE REGION	AVERAGE EFFICIENCY RATE (PERCENTAGE)	OPERATION AND MAINTENANCE COST (MILLS/KILOWATT-HOUR)	CAPITAL COST ($/KILOWATT)
1	91.40	5.7	493
2	91.80	5.2	626
3	92.40	4.7	304
4	91.40	5.0	262
5	92.30	4.3	361
6	92.50	4.6	228
7	91.20	5.5	354
8	88.30	5.6	309
9	90.80	5.3	514
10	91.00	5.6	279

TABLES 14, 15, 16 AND 17 SHOW AGGREGATE HEAT RATES FOR EXISTING EQUIPMENT FOR BASE, CYCLING, DAILY PEAK AND SEASONAL PEAK LOADS, RESPECTIVELY. TABLE 18 SHOWS HEAT RATES* FOR NEW FACILITIES (SAME FOR EACH REGION), AND TABLE 19 SHOWS HEAT VALUES FOR FOSSIL FUELS. THE RATIO OF HEAT RATE TO HEAT VALUE DETERMINES THE AMOUNT OF FUEL NEEDED TO GENERATE ONE KILOWATT. SPECIFICALLY, THE FUEL REQUIRED TO OPERATE A PLANT TO GENERATE ONE MEGAWATT OF ELECTRICITY IN A PARTICULAR LOAD (I.E. BASE, CYCLING, DAILY PEAK OR SEASONAL PEAK) IS:

FUEL REQUIREMENT = (HEAT RATE)/(HEAT VALUE)

WHERE THE AMOUNT OF FUEL REQUIRED IS MEASURED IN PHYSICAL UNITS (I.E. TONS, BARRELS, THOUSANDS OF STANDARD CUBIC FEET, ETC.)

TABLE 20 SHOWS NUCLEAR FUEL SUPPLY DATA.

* THE HEAT RATE IS THE ENERGY REQUIRED PER HOUR OF OPERATION, WHERE ENERGY IS MEASURED BY BRITISH THERMAL UNITS (BTU)

TABLE 14: HEAT RATES FOR EXISTING EQUIPMENT OPERATED IN BASE LOAD
(BTU PER KILOWATT-HOUR)

PLANT TYPE	DOE REGION									
	1	2	3	4	5	6	7	8	9	10
RESIDUAL-FIRED STEAM	10000	10300	10700	10000	12100	10300	11200	14500	9800	11000
DISTILLATE-FIRED SIMPLE CYCLE	14500	14600	12500	13000	14500	12800	12500	12000	15700	12800
DISTILLATE-FIRED COMBINED CYCLE	8500	8500	8500	8500	8500	8500	8500	-	8500	8500
GAS-FIRED STEAM	12500	10900	10900	11100	13400	10100	11300	11900	10400	11500
GAS-FIRED TURBINE	14000	15400	14300	16500	14700	13000	14700	12200	13700	12600
BITUMINOUS COAL (WITH SCRUBBER)	10510	11000	10300	10300	10500	-	10900	11600	10700	-
BITUMINOUS COAL (WITHOUT SCRUBBER)	10110	10500	9900	9900	10200	-	10500	11200	10300	-
SUB-BITUMINOUS COAL	-	-	-	-	10300	10100	10600	10700	-	10700
LIGNITE	-	-	-	-	12400	10500	-	11900	-	-

TABLE 15: HEAT RATES FOR EXISTING EQUIPMENT OPERATED IN CYCLING LOAD
(BTU PER KILOWATT-HOUR)

PLANT TYPE	DOE REGION									
	1	2	3	4	5	6	7	8	9	10
RESIDUAL-FIRED STEAM	10500	10800	11200	10500	12600	10800	11700	15000	10300	11500
DISTILLATE-FIRED SIMPLE CYCLE	14500	15100	13000	13500	15000	13300	13000	12500	16200	12500
DISTILLATE-FIRED COMBINED CYCLE	9000	9000	9000	9000	9000	9000	9000	-	9000	9000
GAS-FIRED STEAM	13000	11400	11400	11600	13900	10600	11800	12400	10900	12000
GAS-FIRED TURBINE	14500	15900	14800	17000	15200	13500	15200	12700	14200	13100
BITUMINOUS COAL (WITH SCRUBBER)	11000	11500	10800	10800	11000	-	11400	12100	11200	-
BITUMINOUS COAL (WITHOUT SCRUBBER)	10600	11000	10400	10400	10700	-	11000	11700	10800	-
SUB-BITUMINOUS COAL	-	-	-	-	10800	10600	11100	11200	-	11200
LIGNITE	-	-	-	-	12900	11000	-	12400	-	-

TABLE 16: HEAT RATES FOR EXISTING EQUIPMENT OPERATED IN DAILY PEAK LOAD
(BTU PER KILOWATT-HOUR)

PLANT TYPE	DOE REGION									
	1	2	3	4	5	6	7	8	9	10
RESIDUAL-FIRED STEAM	10500	10800	11200	10500	12600	10800	11700	15000	10300	11500
DISTILLATE-FIRED SIMPLE CYCLE	14500	15100	13000	13500	15000	13300	13000	12500	16200	12500
DISTILLATE-FIRED COMBINED CYCLE	9000	9000	9000	9000	9000	9000	9000	-	9000	9000
GAS-FIRED STEAM	13000	11400	11400	11600	13900	10600	11800	12400	10900	12000
GAS-FIRED TURBINE	14500	15900	14800	17000	15200	13500	15200	12700	14200	13100
BITUMINOUS COAL (WITH SCRUBBER)	11000	11500	10800	10800	11000	-	11400	12100	11200	-
BITUMINOUS COAL (WITHOUT SCRUBBER)	10600	11000	10400	10400	10700	-	11000	11700	10800	-
SUB-BITUMINOUS COAL	-	-	-	-	10800	10600	11100	11200	-	11200
LIGNITE	-	-	-	-	12900	11000	-	12400	-	-

TABLE 17: HEAT RATES FOR EXISTING EQUIPMENT OPERATED IN SEASONAL PEAK LOAD
(BTU PER KILOWATT-HOUR)

PLANT TYPE	DOE REGION									
	1	2	3	4	5	6	7	8	9	10
RESIDUAL-FIRED STEAM										
DISTILLATE-FIRED SIMPLE CYCLE	14500	15100	13000	13500	15000	13300	13000	12500	16200	12500
DISTILLATE-FIRED COMBINED CYCLE	-	-	-	-	-	-	-	-	-	-
GAS-FIRED STEAM	-	-	-	-	-	-	-	-	-	-
GAS-FIRED TURBINE	14500	15900	14800	17000	15200	13500	15200	12700	14200	13100
BITUMINOUS COAL (WITH SCRUBBER)	-	-	-	-	-	-	-	-	-	-
BITUMINOUS COAL (WITHOUT SCRUBBER)	-	-	-	-	-	-	-	-	-	-
SUB-BITUMINOUS COAL	-	-	-	-	-	-	-	-	-	-
LIGNITE	-	-	-	-	-	-	-	-	-	-

TABLE 18: HEAT RATES FOR NEW EQUIPMENT
(MILLIONS OF BTU PER KILOWATT)

PLANT TYPE	BASE	CYCLING	DAILY PEAK	SEASONAL PEAK
RESIDUAL-FIRED STEAM	9650	10300	10300	-
DISTILLATE-FIRED SIMPLE CYCLE	9000	9500	9500	9750
DISTILLATE-FIRED COMBINED CYCLE	7000	7500	7500	-
GAS-FIRED STEAM	10010	10760	10760	-
GAS-FIRED TURBINE	9000	9500	9500	9750
BITUMINOUS COAL (WITH SCRUBBER)	9840	10300	10300	-
BITUMINOUS COAL (WITHOUT SCRUBBER)	9870	10350	10350	-
SUB-BITUMINOUS COAL	10230	10710	10710	-
LIGNITE	10500	11000	11000	-

TABLE 19: HEAT VALUES OF FOSSIL FUELS
(MILLIONS OF BTU PER PHYSICAL UNITS)

FUEL	HEAT VALUE	PHYSICAL UNITS
RESIDUAL OIL	6.287	BARRELS
DISTILLATE OIL	5.825	BARRELS
NATURAL GAS	1.032	THOUSANDS OF STANDARD CUBIC FEET
COAL	22.500	TONS

TABLE 20: NUCLEAR FUEL SUPPLY CURVE

INCREMENTAL CAPACITY SUPPORTED (MEGAWATTS)	COSTS (1975 MILLS/KWH)
79.0	6.04
46.0	6.29
40.0	6.41
12.0	6.53
13.0	6.90
15.0	7.15

REFERENCES

1. *Annual Report to Congress 1977.* Energy Information Administration, U.S. Department of Energy, Washington, D.C., 1977.
2. Atkinson, A. B., and L. Waverman, "Resource Allocation and the Regulated Firm: Comment," *Bell Journal of Economics, 4,* 1973.
3. Averch, H., and L. L. Johnson, "Behavior of the Firm Under Regulation Constraint," *American Economic Review, 52,* Dec. 1962.
4. Aymond, A. H, "Comment" on "Reassessment of Economic Standards for Rate of Return Under Regulations," in *Rate of Return Under Regulation: New Directions* and Perspectives, Michigan State University Public Utility Studies (Harry M. Trebing, and R. Hayden Howard, eds.). East Lansing, Mich., 1969.
5. Bailey, E. E., *Economic Theory of Regulatory Constraint.* Lexington, Mass.: Heath, 1973.
6. Bailey, E. E., and J. C. Malone, "Resource Allocation and the Regulated Firm," *Bell Journal of Economics, 1,* 1970.
7. Baughman, M. L., P. L. Joskow, and D. P. Kamat, *Electric Power in the United States: Models and Policy Analysis.* Cambridge, Mass.: M.I.T. Press, 1979.
8. Baumol, W. J., and A. K. Klevorick, "Input Choices and Rate of Return Regulation: An Overview," *Bell Journal of Economics, 1,* 1970.
9. *Bluefield Water Works vs. West Virginia Public Service Commission,* 262 U.S. 679, 1923.
10. Bonbright, J. C., *Principles of Public Utility Rates.* New York: Columbia University Press, 1961.
11. Boyes, W. J., "An Empirical Examination of the Averch-Johnson Effect," *Economic Inquiry, 14,* 1976.
12. Burness, H. S., W. D. Montgomery, and J. P. Quirk, "The Turnkey Era in Nuclear Power: A Case Study in Risk Sharing Arrangements Involving Regulated Firms," *Social Science Working Paper 175.* Pasadena, Ca.: California Institute of Technology, 1977.
13. Cazalet, E. G., C. E. Clark, and T. W. Keelin, "Costs and Benefits of Over/Under Capacity in Electric Power System Planning," *Electric Power Research Institute Research Project EA-972.* Electric Power Research Institute, Pasadena, Ca. Oct. 1978.
14. Conrad, C. A., "Comment" on "Fair Rate of Return and Incentives—Some General Considerations," in *Performance Under Regulation,* Michigan State University Public Utilities Studies (Harry M. Trebing, ed.). East Lansing, Mich., 1968.
15. Courville, L., "Regulation and Efficiency in the Electric Utility Industry," *Bell Journal of Economics, 6,* 1975.
16. Cowing, T. G., "The Effectiveness of Rate-of-Return Regulation: An Empirical Test Using Profit Functions," in *Production Economics: A Dual Approach to Theory and Applications,* Vol. 2 (M. Fuss and D. McFadden, eds.). Amsterdam: North-Holland, 1978.
17. Cramton, R. C., "The Effectiveness of Economic Regulation: A Legal View," *American Economic Review, 54,* 1964.
18. Day, J. T., "Forecasting Minimum Production Costs with Linear Programming," *Institute of Electrical and Electronic Engineers Power and Systems, IEEE PAS 90-2.* 1971.

19. Emery, E. D., "Regulated Utilities and Equipment Manufacturers' Conspiracies in the Electrical Power Industry," *Bell Journal of Economics*, 4, 1973.
20. "Electric Load Forecasting Probing Issues with Models," *Energy Modeling Forum No. 3*. Stanford, Calif.: Stanford University, April 1979.
21. Farris, M. T., and R. J. Sampson, *Public Utilities: Regulation, Management and Ownership*. Boston: Houghton Mifflin, 1973.
22. *Federal Power Commission vs. Hope Natural Gas Company*, 320 U.S. 591, 1944.
23. *Federal Power Commission vs. Natural Gas Pipeline Company of America*, 315 U.S. 575, 1942.
24. "Respecification of PIES Electric Utility Model," General Electric Co., Center for Energy Systems, Schenectady, N.Y., April 30, 1976.
25. Greenberg, H. J., "A Lagrangian Property for Homogeneous Programs," *Journal of Optimization Theory and Applications*, *12*, July, 1973.
26. Hayashi, P. M., and J. M. Trapani, "Rate of Return Regulation and the Regulated Firm's Choice of Capital-Labor Ratio: Further Empirical Evidence on the Averch-Johnson Model," *Southern Economic Journal*, *42*, 1976.
27. Jaffee, B. L., "Depreciation in a Simple Regulatory Model," *Bell Journal of Economics*, 4, 1973.
28. Johnson, L. L., "Behavior of the Firm Under Regulatory Constraint: A Reassessment," *American Economic Review*, *63*, 1973.
29. Joskow, P., "Inflation and Environmental Concern: Structural Change in the Process of Public Utility Price Regulation," *Journal of Law and Economics*, Oct. 1974. Vol. 17.
30. Kahn, A. E., "The Graduated Fair Return: Comment, *American Economic Review*, *58*, 1966.
31. Kahn, A. E., "Between Theory and Practice: Reflections of a Neophyte Public Utility Regulator," *Public Utilities Fortnightly*, Jan. 1975. Vol. 95.
32. Lerner, A. P., "Conflicting Principles of Public Utility Rate Regulation," *Journal of Law and Economics*, 1964. Vol. 12.
33. Leventhal, H., "Vitality of the Comparable Earnings Standard for Regulation of Utilities in a Growth Economy," *Yale Law Journal*, *74*, No. 6, May 1965.
34. Massé, P., and R. Gibrat, "Applications of Linear Programming to Investments in the Electric Power Industry," *Management Science*, *3*, 1957.
35. Massel, M. S., "The Regulatory Process and Public Utility Performance," *Performance Under Regulation*, Michigan State University Public Utility Studies (Harry M. Trebing, ed.). East Lansing, Mich., 1968.
36. *McCardle vs. Indianapolis Water Company*, 272 U.S. 400, 1926.
37. McKay, D. J., *Two Essays on the Economics of Electricity Supply: 1. Has the Averch-Johnson Effect Been Empirically Verified? 2. Electricity Pricing*, Dissertation, Pasadena, Ca.: California Institute of Technology, Aug. 1977.
38. McNicol, D. L., "The Comparative Statics Properties of the Theory of the Regulated Firm," *Bell Journal of Economics and Management Sciences*, 4, 1973.
39. *1977 Annual Report*. National Association of Regulatory Utility Commissioners.
40. Olsen, C. E., "Public Utility Regulation in Practice and Its Impact on Electricity Demand and Production," in *Studies in Electric Utility Regulation* (C. J. Cicchetti, ed.). Cambridge, Mass.: Ballinger Publishing Company, 1975.
41. Ostergren, C. N., "Is the Averch-Johnson Theory Tenable," *Public Utilities Fortnightly*, *95*, Jan. 1975.

42. Petersen, H. C., "An Empirical Test of Regulatory Effects," *Bell Journal of Economics*, 6, 1975.

43. Posner, R. A., "Measuring the Success of Regulation in Terms of Its Economic Effects," *Stanford Law Review*, Feb. 1969.

44. Posner, R. A., "Theories of Economic Regulation," *Bell Journal of Economics*, 5, Autumn 1974.

45. Rockafellar, R. T., *Convex Analysis*. Princeton, N.J.: Princeton University Press, 1970.

46. Sanghvi, A., and D. Limaye, "Planning for Electrical Generation Capacity in the Pacific Northwest: A Decision Analysis of the Costs of Over-and-Under Building," *Energy Policy*, 7, 1979.

47. Schiffel, D., "Electric Utility Regulation: An Overview of Fuel Adjustment Clauses," *Public Utilities Fortnightly*, 95, June 1975.

48. *Smyth vs. Ames*, 169 U.S. 466, 1898.

49. *Southwestern Bell Telephone Company vs. Public Service Commission of Missouri*, 262 U.S. 276, 291, 1923.

50. Soyster, A. L., "Project Independence Evaluation System (PIES) Utility Model Validation." Blacksburg, Va.: Virginia Polytechnic Institute, 1979.

51. Spann, R. M., "Rate of Return Regulation and Efficiency in Production—An Empirical Test of Averch-Johnson Thesis," *Bell Journal of Economics*, 5, 1974.

52. *Statistical Yearbook of the Electric Utility Industry*. Washington, D.C.: Edison Electric Institute, 1978.

53. Stigler, G. J., "The Theory of Economic Regulation," *Bell Journal of Economics*, 2, Spring 1971.

54. Stigler, G. J., and C. Friedland, "What Can Regulators Regulate? The Case of Electricity," *Journal of Law and Economics*, 5, Oct. 1962.

55. Stoner, R. D., and S. C. Peck, "The Diffusion of Technological Innovations Among Privately-Owned Electric Utilities, 1950–1975," *NTIS (PB-277 371)*. Washington, D.C.: U.S. Department of Commerce.

56. Takayama, A., "Behavior of the Firm Under Regulatory Constraint," *American Economic Review*, 59, 1969.

57. Turvey, R., *Optimal Pricing and Investment in Electricity*. Cambridge, Mass.: M.I.T. Press, 1968.

58. Wein, H. H., "Fair Rate of Return and Incentives—Some General Considerations," *Performance Under Regulation*, Michigan State University Public Utility Studies (Harry M. Trebing, ed.). East Lansing, Mich., 1968.

59. Wellisz, S. H., "Regulation of Natural Gas Pipeline Companies: An Economic Analysis," *Journal of Political Economy*, 71, 1963.

60. West, D. A., and A. A. Eubank, Jr., "An Automatic Cost of Capital Adjustment Model for Regulating Public Utilities," *Financial Management*, 5, 1976.

61. *Wilcox vs. Consolidated Gas Company*, 212 U.S. 19 (1909).

62. Williamson, O. E., "Peak Load Pricing and Optimal Capacity Under Indivisibility Constraint," *American Economic Review*, 56, 1966.

63. Zajac, E. E., "A Geometric Treatment of Averch-Johnson's Behavior of the Firm Model," *American Economic Review*, 70, 1970.

64. Zajac, E. E., "Note on 'Gold Plating' or 'Rate Base Padding'," *Bell Journal of Economics*, 3, 1972.

65. Ziemba, W. T., "The Behavior of a Firm Subject to Stochastic Regulatory Review: Comment," *Bell Journal of Economics*, 5, 1974.

SUGGESTED READINGS

Bailey, E. E., "Peak Load Pricing Regulatory Constraint," *Journal of Political Economy*, *80*, 1972.

Bailey, E. E., and R. D. Coleman, "The Effect of Lagged Regulation in an Averch-Johnson, Model," *Bell Journal of Economics*, 2, 1972.

Clemens, E. W., *Economics and Public Utilities*, New York: Appleton, 1950.

Davis, B. E., and F. T. Sparrow, "Valuation Models in Regulation," *Bell Journal of Economics*, *3*, 1972.

Gordon, M. J., "Some Estimates of the Cost of Capital to the Electric Utility Industry, 1955–1957: Comment," *American Economic Review*, *57*, 1967.

Hilton, G. J., "The Basic Behavior of Regulatory Commissions," *American Economic Review*, *63*, 1963.

Jorgenson, D., and S. Handel, "Investment Behavior in U.S. Regulated Utilities," *Bell Journal of Economics*, 2, 1971.

Kahn, A. E., "Inducements to Superior Performance Price," in *Performance Under Regulation*, Michigan State University Public Utility Studies (Harry M. Trebing, ed.). East Lansing, Mich., 1968.

Klevorick, A. K., "The 'Optimal' Fair Rate of Return," *Bell Journal of Economics*, 2, 1971.

Miller, M., and F. Modigliani, "Some Estimates of the Cost of Capital to the Electric Utility Industry, 1954–1957," *American Economic Review*, 56, 1966.

Murphy, F. H., and A. L. Soyster, The Averch-Johnson Model with Leontief Production Functions: Extensions and Applications, Energy Economics, 4, No. 3, Butterworth & Co., London, July 1982.

Myers, S. C., "The Application of Finance Theory to Public Utility Rate Cases," *Bell Journal of Economics*, *3*, 1972.

Nguyen, D. T., and G. J. MacGregor-Reid, "Interdependent Demands Regulatory Constraint and Peak Load Pricing," *Journal of Industrial Economics*, *25*, 1977.

Solomon, E., "Alternative Rate of Return Concepts and Their Implications for Utility Regulation," *Bell Journal of Economics*, *1*, 1970.

Soyster, A. L., and R. T. Eynon, "The Conceptual Basis for Modelling the Electric Utilities Sub-Model of Project Independence Evaluation System," *Applied Mathematical Modelling*, *3*, 1979.

Steiner, P. O., "Peak Loads and Efficient Pricing," *Quarterly Journal of Economics*, *71*, 1957.